523 HARD
TO BELIEVE
FACTS

by

Nayden Kostov

523 HARD TO BELIEVE FACTS

by

Nayden Kostov

Luxembourg
2019

523 HARD TO BELIEVE FACTS

first edition

Author:	Nayden Kostov
Editor:	Andrea Leitenberger
Format:	5,25 x 8

ISBN: 978-99959-980-9-7

CONTENTS

PROLOGUE

I admit that most trivia books are insufferably boring. This book, however, is loaded with fun and verified facts, presented in a manner that will provide you with hours of entertainment. It will charge you with never-ending intellectual ammunition for a lifetime of parties. If you argue that it is useless information, you will be right until you know how to use it. Amaze your friends and family by telling them that, so far, every bearded US president has been a Republican or that female ferrets need to have sex at least once a year, otherwise, they risk dying of estrogen poisoning!

Following the success of my trivia website RaiseYourBrain, I published "1123 Hard to Believe Facts", which was read by tens of thousands of people and accumulated hundreds of 5-star reviews on Amazon and GoodReads. "853 Hard to Believe Facts" followed and was even more successful. As the third instalment of this series, "523 Hard to Believe Facts" has more detail for each fact, as requested by previous readers.

This book can be fun for high school students too: even the most "spicy" entries, neatly separated in the chapter "Facts about human and animal sexuality", remain factual and abstain from profanity. To my greatest delight, an avid reader of my website explained that he was preparing daily fact sheets for his son's lunch box. He prints out three facts every day to create some lunchtime fun for his child and provoke his intellectual curiosity. Honestly, I wish my parents had done the same for me!

CHAPTER I

Myth vs Fact

1.

The number of moles is a good indicator of skin cancer.

It has been disproved. Additionally, recent studies claim that the more moles you have, the longer you live.

2.

Music lessons improve math results.

It is a myth. Taking music lessons simply means that you come from a richer family. Richer kids are known to have better access to private tutors and good quality education.

3.

The US state of Colorado is a rectangle.

Wrong. It has 697 "sides", making it a *hexahectaenneacontakaiheptagon*.

4.
The anchor stops the ship.

Actually, it is the weight of the chain and its friction with the sea bottom.

5.
The piece of opera "Aida" was commissioned to commemorate the Suez Channel.

Wrong. "Aida" was commissioned from Giuseppe Verdi to celebrate the opening of the Opera House in Cairo in early 1871. The Suez Canal had already opened in 1869. "Aida", however, was not the opening opera. The scenery and costumes being made in Paris, France, did not make it in time to Cairo, Egypt.

6.
The polygraph test is a lie detector.

Technically speaking, it is just an arousal detector.

7.
All characters in The Simpsons TV series have four fingers.

There is one exception: God has five.

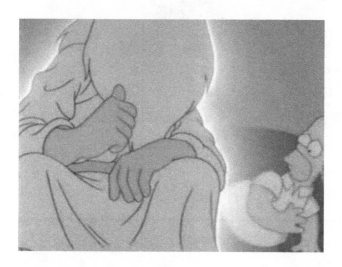

8.

It is OK to share a picture of the Eiffel Tower at night while illuminated.

It turns out the light show at night was added in 1985 and is still protected under French copyright law as an artistic work. Technically, it is illegal to share, sell, or publish photos and videos of the night-lit Eiffel Tower without prior permission from the *Société d'Exploitation de la Tour Eiffel.*

9.

Birds of prey use their sharp hooked beak for defence and attack.

They mostly use their strong feet and talons.

10.

If you are a citizen of Monaco, you can go to the famous Casino in Monaco and gamble.

Actually, it is only allowed if you are a foreigner.

11.

Tesla Model S is a zero-emissions all-electric vehicle and enjoys tax rebates worldwide.

Not everywhere: in 2016, a Tesla owner in Singapore was fined more than 10,000 US dollars for excessive emissions. Due to the local methodology of calculating CO_2 emissions equivalent, the car was deemed too polluting.

12.

If your guests say the wine tastes like a cat's pee, they are being rude.

Do not be too quick: in wine tasting, a "cat-pee aroma" can be a compliment.

13.

Divers suffer from nitrogen narcosis.

While this is correct, few people know that breathing pure oxygen at depths more than 6 m (20 ft) can be lethal.

14.

"Kangaroo" was an answer meaning "I do not understand you" when newly arriving Europeans asked the Australian Aboriginal people about the strange animal.

This proved to be a myth. "Kangaroo" was the word designating this animal in one of the local languages.

15.

Greece is a southern country and its capital, Athens, is further south than foggy Tokyo, Japan.

It is exactly the opposite. Check a map.

16.

Jupiter orbits the Sun.

Wrong. The gas giant is so big that its centre of mass with the Sun, or barycentre, lies 1.07 solar radii from the middle of the Sun – or 7 percent of a Sun-radius above the Sun's surface. Both the Sun and Jupiter orbit around that point in space.

17.

The practice of selling one's kidney for profit is illegal everywhere.

In Iran, **it is legal** and regulated by the government. In any given year, it is estimated that 1,400 Iranians sell one of their kidneys to a recipient who was previously unknown to them. Iran is currently the only country in the world that allows the sale of one's kidney for compensation (typically a payment). Consequently, the country does not have either a waiting list or a shortage of available organs.

18.

When you are in an aeroplane and experience a hard landing, it is due to poor pilot skills.

Not always: if the runway is covered in water, the aircraft has to touch down hard to avoid aquaplaning.

19.

The dark side of the Moon is always dark.

Wrong. It was called the "dark" side because it was not visible from Earth and hence unknown, not because sunlight does not reach it. In the very beginning of 2019, a Chinese spacecraft became the first to land on the dark side of the Moon.

20.
Tajikistan is the country with the largest Tajik population.

Wrong: more Tajiks live in Afghanistan than within Tajikistan. Tajikistan has a population of 8.7 million people, of which around 7.5 million are ethnic Tajiks; in Afghanistan, there are somewhere between 9 and 11 million Tajiks.

21.
Lobsters have always been an expensive delicacy we know today.

Wrong: before the mid-19th century, lobsters were fed routinely to US prisoners, apprentices, slaves, and children. In Massachusetts, USA, some servants sought to avoid lobster-heavy diets by including stipulations in their contracts that they would only be served the shellfish twice a week. Locals used the massive pile of "cockroaches of the sea" as they used to call them, as fertilisers and fish bait.

22.
Many US schools are handing out perfect-attendance certificates as a way to motivate students to show up and it works.

It is just not working. In 2014, researchers at Harvard, UCLA, and Stanford (USA), set up an elaborate experiment with more than 15,000 middle and high school students in California during the 2015-16 school year. Instead of boosting attendance, the certificates either did nothing or reduced attendance. Among students who were told about being eligible for perfect-attendance certificates ahead of time, their attendance did not budge. However, students who received the certificates as a surprise reward for their prior record subsequently started actually missing more days of school than a control group of students who were not eligible for the certificates.

23.
The Mississippi river is longer than the Missouri.

The opposite is true. Although it is longer by just a little bit, the Missouri is considered a tributary to the Mississippi.

24.

On a standard geographical map, Greenland appears more or less the size of Africa.

In reality, Africa is 14 times as large.

25.
Robots are a recent creation.

In fact, the first robot was created much earlier than what most people think. A steam-powered "pigeon" was created around 400 to 350 BCE by the ancient Greek mathematician Archytas. This robo-bird was made out of wood and used steam to power its movements. It could fly about 200 meters (600 ft) before running out of steam.

26.
Joseph Stalin's words "The death of one person is a tragedy, but the death of one million is a statistic" are tasteless and wrong.

Unfortunately, he was somehow right. Psychologists have repeatedly found that people experience a greater emotional reaction to one death than to many, even if the circumstances are identical. Perversely, the more victims, the less sympathy people feel. The effect even has a name: collapse of compassion. It is not that we cannot care about a million deaths, psychologists believe: instead, we fear being overwhelmed and switch off our emotions in pre-emptive self-defence.

27.

The fidget spinner – the toy everyone wanted in 2017 – was invented fairly recently.

Actually, it was patented back in 1993.

28.

Bees have two eyes.

Bees have five eyes. The two big eyes on a bee are called compound eyes because they are made up of thousands of tiny lenses. Each lens (called a *facet*) sees a small part of a scene and, all together, the lenses form an entire picture. You can compare it to a tile mosaic where tiles of different colours are put together to form a picture. The three other eyes are called simple eyes or *ocelli*. They are at the top of the bee's head in a triangular pattern and are very small. These eyes do not see images but can detect light, especially changes in light.

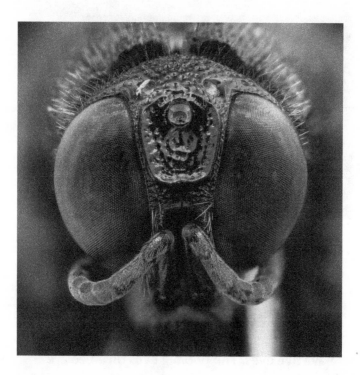

CHAPTER II

Unbelievable facts about virtually everything

1.

Some airlines forbid their pilots from growing beards. The reason is that an oxygen mask should fit tightly on the face if an emergency situation occurs, and a beard could prevent this.

2.

In 2017, Saudi Arabia became the first country to give citizenship to a robot. Her name is Sophia.

3.

In 2018, Emile Ratelband, a Dutchman aged 69, petitioned the courts to allow him to identify as 20 years younger on the grounds – among other things – that it would yield him more matches on Tinder.

The court rejected his attempt.

4.

The number of teenagers in a car proportionally increases the chances of having a car accident.

5.

Singapore has four official languages from four different linguistic families: English, Mandarin Chinese, Malay, and Tamil.

6.

In Sweden, a *Speed Camera Lottery* rewards drivers who obey the speed limit with the money raised through fining those who exceed it.

7.

The only member of ZZ Top who did not have a beard was Frank... Beard! He has sported a goatee since 2013.

8.

The French Fencing Federation recognised lightsabre duelling as a sport in early 2019.

9.

There are mountains with the colours of the rainbow at several locations worldwide. The most popular are those in Peru and China.

10.

The notorious US gangster, Al Capone, was the first to call for putting expiration dates on milk bottles. After his niece had become extremely ill due to drinking bad milk, the influential Chicago mobster lobbied aggressively for expiration dates to be put on milk for the safety of children and pregnant women.

11.

In Luxembourg, it is illegal to defrost your car by keeping the engine running while the car is stationary.

12.

In Thailand, touching the queen was punishable by death. In 1880, the queen drowned as no-one dared to save her when she fell in the water from the royal boat. Numerous witnesses watched her drown and did not dare to help.

13.

The 2003 World Aquatics Championship took place in Barcelona, Spain. It will be remembered as the first time when the medals were filled with water.

14.

If you fold a piece of paper 42 times, it will be so thick that it could reach the Moon.

15.

Helen Adams Keller (1880-1968) was a US author and political activist. She became the first deaf-blind person worldwide to earn a Bachelor of Arts degree.

16.

Initially, Coca-Cola was intended to serve as a cure for morphine addiction and, until 1903, contained cocaine.

17.

In the 1970s and early 1980s, Nauru was the richest country per capita. All essential services used to be free, and there was no taxation. Now, it is among the five poorest countries in the world. They became rich due to bird poo (*guano*), and now, they are poor because their source of wealth has been depleted and savings lost due to corruption.

18.

Hungarian Károly Takács was the first to win two Olympic gold medals in the 25-metre rapid-fire pistol event. He did that with his left hand. This would hardly be a surprising fact, but we have to take into account that he was right-handed and learned how to shoot with his left hand only after his right one was seriously injured.

19.

In South Korea, only blind masseurs can obtain a licence to practice. The law was established in 1912 when Korea was under Japanese colonial rule to help guarantee the blind a livelihood. South Korea's Constitutional Court has defended the law on several occasions, most recently in 2018.

20.

In 2017, a test proved that the Audi TT sports car accelerates faster when towed by a Tesla Model X, rather than when using its own engine and wheels.

21.

The Capture of the Dutch fleet at Den Helder on the night of 23 January 1795 presents a rare occurrence of a "naval" battle between warships and cavalry, in which a French Revolutionary Hussar regiment surprised a Dutch Republican fleet frozen at anchor between the 3-km (1.9 mi) stretch of sea that separates the mainland port of Den Helder and the island of Texel. After a charge across the frozen Zuiderzee, the French cavalry captured 14 Dutch ships and 850 guns.

22.

A *carat* is a unit of mass equal to 0.2 g (0.007 oz) used for measuring gemstones. Maybe you never thought about that, but a carat is a metric unit with no imperial equivalent.

23.

Statistically speaking, women named Eleanor are 100 times more likely to get into Oxford University than women called Jade.

24.

Saint Martin is an island in the northeast Caribbean Sea, approximately 300 km (190 mi) east of Puerto Rico. It has been divided between France and the Netherlands since 1648. The French half of the island is part of the European Union; the Dutch one is not.

25.

At the end of the American Civil War, some 20,000 Confederates fled to Brazil, where slavery was legal and formed a community known as "Confederados".

26.

In the first years after its invention, basketball was played using a real basket that did not have a hole in the bottom part, so the ball had to be taken out of the basket after each score.

27.

The most remote island in the world is Bouvet Island, a small and uninhabited island in the South Atlantic Ocean that is a dependency of Norway. The nearest land is the uninhabited Queen Maud Land, Antarctica, over 1,600 km (994 mi) to the south. The closest inhabited lands are Tristan da Cunha, 2,260 km (1,404 mi) away, and the coast of South Africa, 2,580 km (1,603 mi) away.

28.

The Toyota MR2 had to be sold under a different
name in France since "MR2" sounds like the
word for "shitty".

29.

The longest French border is with Brazil.

30.

The Russian authorities forbade 2018 Football World
Cup fans from bringing live chickens to matches.

31.

You visualise the flow of time the same way you read
(left to right for the Western world).

32.

In case you ever wondered, bears always win against lions in organised fights. Ancient Romans tested it on multiple occasions.

33.

Champagne corks were first used in France around 1665.

34.

Praying mantises are capable of capturing birds and fish and eating them.

35.

Batology is the scientific study of plants in the genus *Rubus*, commonly known as brambles: raspberries, blackberries, and dewberries.

36.

There is a high chance that your favourite chewing gum contains *lanolin*: a waxy secretion from sheep's skin.

37.

As of early 2019, China is the largest importer of industrial robots.

38.

In their lifetime, elephants have six sets of molars. When a tooth wears out, another pushes forward to replace it. Sadly, the loss of teeth is the leading cause of death among mature elephants.

39.

The lighter is older than the match. The first gas lighter was invented in 1823 by the famous German chemist, Johann Wolfgang Dobereiner. English chemist, John Walker, created the first friction match in 1826.

40.

Platinum can turn snails into slugs. During embryogenesis of the freshwater snail, *Marisa cornuarietis*, the exposure to platinum results in the formation of an internal shell instead of the habitual external shell.

41.

George Weah is the first and only African footballer to have won the prestigious *Ballon d'Or* award for best player in the world. By the way, he became the 25th President of Liberia in early 2018.

42.

In Iceland, the production of vegetables and fruit in greenhouses is a rapidly growing sector. This includes the commercial production of bananas.

43.

There are some 25 million stray dogs in India. This is considered the largest population of predator mammals in the world.

44.

During the Indo-Pakistani War of 1947, the British king George VI was the head of state of both warring nations. In a legal sense, he was waging war against himself.

45.

In 2017, a Russian naval spy ship sank in the Black Sea off Turkey's coast. The reason was rather trivial: it hit a Togo-flagged vessel transporting livestock.

46.

Sergei Shtemenko was a Soviet general who served as the Chief of the Soviet Armed Forces' General Staff in the period 1948-1952. He is the only person to be promoted to the rank of General of the Army three times (he was demoted twice in his career).

47.

Peter Freuchen (1886-1957) was a Danish explorer of the Arctic region. On one occasion, to free himself from an avalanche, he formed a dagger from his faeces to carve through ice and snow.

48.

Jack Daniel, the founder of the whiskey distillery of the same name, died from blood poisoning in 1911. The infection started in one of Jack's toes that he injured when he forgot his safe's combination and started kicking the safe in anger.

49.

Worldwide, Italy has the largest parliament, with almost 1,000 members. It is one of the few legislatures in the world to reserve seats in both houses of its parliament for citizens residing abroad. There are altogether eighteen such seats.

50.

For nearly two centuries, the Fugate family of Kentucky, USA, remained isolated from the outside world and passed their hereditary blue skin colour from generation to generation.

51.

Jessica Allen decided to become a surrogate mother in 2016. The US woman became pregnant with her biological child while carrying the other baby. Only after a lengthy legal battle did she eventually get custody of her own son.

52.

A Romanian man named Constantin Reliu was registered officially as deceased by his wife in 2013 while he was working abroad. He recently tried without any success to convince a Romanian court that he was still alive. The court refused to annul his death certificate.

53.

In the 1950s, Chrysler designed the Chrysler TV-8 tank. It was intended to be a nuclear-powered medium tank capable of land and amphibious warfare. It never saw mass production.

54.

It has been proven that many dementia patients have increased creativity.

55.

Redheads can produce their own personal supply of Vitamin D. This means that ginger-haired people are significantly less likely to develop rickets or contract tuberculosis.

56.

Statistically speaking, you will be better off financially at the age of 40 if you were born slightly more intelligent than average, rather than slightly richer than average.

57.

The highest consumer of chocolate per capita is Switzerland. In 2015, every Swiss resident ate on average 9 kg (20 pounds).

58.

The University of Bologna, Italy, was founded in 1088 and is the oldest university in continuous operation in Europe.

59.

There was a documented case when the Ebola virus changed the colour of a patient's eyes from blue to green.

60.
Emmanuel Jean-Michel Frédéric Macron (born in 1977) is a French politician serving as President of the French Republic since 2017. Macron's wife is almost 25 years older than him, and one of his stepchildren is two years older than him.

61.
The famous scientist, Nikola Tesla, invented wireless charging more than a century ago.

62.

"E Depois do Adeus" was the Portuguese entry in the 1974 Eurovision Song Contest. The song served as one of the two signals to launch the Carnation Revolution in Portugal against the regime of the dictator, Marcelo Caetano.

63.

Since 2011, inmates in several federal prisons in Brazil get four days off their sentence for every book they read.

64.

According to a report from mid-2018, over 800 cryptocurrencies launched through initial coin offerings are now considered dead.

65.

In the majority of African countries, work colleagues would only address each other with surnames, and not given names.

66.

The tiny European country of Liechtenstein is the largest producer of false teeth and sausage skins worldwide.

67.

In April 2018, France's highest administrative court upheld a decision to deny citizenship to an Algerian woman for "failing to assimilate". She had refused to shake the hand of the official presiding her 2016 citizenship ceremony.

68.

Treetop-dwelling ants in Southeast Asia have an explosive defensive mechanism: they kill their enemies by blowing themselves up. Also known as "exploding ants", workers in this group respond to threats by deliberately sacrificing themselves, spattering rivals with toxic fluid.

69.

In May 2018, a New York judge ruled that US President, Donald Trump, may not legally block Twitter users from his account based on their political views. It is thought to violate their right to free speech under the First Amendment of the US Constitution.

70.

What do the following sports have in common: Live Pigeon Shooting, Solo Synchronized Swimming, Rope Climb and Tug-of-War? They all used to be official Olympic sports.

71.

The "ugly" animal species tend to be much less the subject of studies than the "cute" ones.

72.

In Japan, you can buy ox tongue-flavoured ice cream.

73.

In 1965, a French lawyer, then 47 years of age, made the following deal with a 90-year-old woman: he would pay her 2,500 francs (about $500) a month until her death and would inherit her apartment. Thirty years later, the lawyer died, having paid more than $184,000. Eventually, Ms Jeanne Calment lived to 122 years and was listed in the Guinness Book of Records.

74.

So far, every bearded US president has been a Republican.

75.

Dancing in public was outlawed in Japan in 1948. Technically today, it is only allowed in clubs that have a special permit.

76.

In Saudi Arabia, there are fashion shows of women's clothes. Instead of female models, however, flying drones display the clothes.

77.

The decimal point was invented in the late 16th century.

78.

The Bank of America was initially called the Bank of Italy.

79.

In France, the energy drink Red Bull was banned until 2008.

80.

There is growing evidence that the dwarf planet, Pluto, has a liquid water ocean underneath its frozen surface.

81.

Lightbulb producer OSRAM's name was derived from the names of two chemical elements: OSmium and WolfRAM (German for tungsten).

82.

Africa is building a belt of trees that will cross the entire continent and 24 countries. *The Great Green Wall of the Sahara and the Sahel Initiative* will change the lives of millions while combatting the global climate crisis.

83.

Bruce Lee was a famous actor and a martial arts champion, but he was also a great boxer: he won the 1958 Hong Kong Inter-School Amateur Boxing Championships. He was also a national dance champion, winning the 1958 Cha-Cha Championship.

84.

In badminton, if your phone rings during a match, you might get a yellow card.

85.

Over the Earth's surface, the ozone layer's average thickness is only about 3 millimetres (1/8 inch).

86.

A baby giraffe grows at the rate of 2.5 cm (one inch) a day.

87.

People with a lower-pitched voice are considered more trustworthy and better leaders. Former British Prime Minister, Margaret Thatcher, was known to have taken lessons to lower her vocal timbre intentionally.

88.

Thomas de Mahy, marquis de Favras (1744-1790), was a French aristocrat and supporter of the Royalist cause during the French Revolution, executed for "planning against the people of France". He is known to have said, "I see that you have made three spelling mistakes" after reading his death sentence.

89.

In 1815, there were numerous rumours in London, UK, that a pig-faced woman was living in the Marylebone city area. Her existence was reported widely as a fact, and countless alleged portraits of her were published. With a belief in pig-faced women commonplace, unscrupulous showmen exhibited living "pig-faced women" at fairs. These were not genuine women, but shaven bears dressed in women's clothing.

90.

The most famous Bulgarian wrestler, Dan Kolov (1892-1940), had around 2,000 fights and won almost all of them (he has only three registered losses in official matches).

91.

Generally speaking, in rich countries, the size of forests is increasing. In Ireland, for instance, in the 1920s, about 1% of the land was woods; a century later, the figure is 11%.

92.

The western German province of Hesse voted in late 2018 to finally scrap the death penalty in a referendum. It fixed a historical oddity, given that capital punishment in Germany was outlawed already in 1949.

93.

On average, office workers click 12 times per minute, which totals 5,760 mouse clicks per 8-hour working day.

94.

"Forty" is the only number we know of in English with its letters in alphabetical order.

95.

According to the World Cancer Research Fund International, the taller you are, the higher the chance to get cancer. Specifically, for every extra 5 cm (2 in) in height, the risk of six cancers is increased as follows: *Kidney cancer*, by 10%; *Pre- and post-menopausal breast cancer*, by 9% and 11% respectively; *Ovarian*, by 8%; *Pancreatic*, by 7%; *Colorectal*, by 5%; and *Prostate cancer*, by 4%.

96.

The famous Italian violinist, Niccolò Paganini, died on 27 May 1840 before a priest could be called. This, along with his widely rumoured association with the devil, made the Church deny his body a Catholic burial in Genoa. His body was buried many years later in Parma, in 1876.

97.

Hippos are not native to Colombia, yet now dozens of feral hippos are bothering Colombian peasants. Where did they come from? They were kept in a private zoo by the notorious drug lord, Pablo Escobar. When the hippos were left behind after his death, they became the largest invasive species in the South American country.

98.
In October 2018, a painting of the anonymous British graffiti artist known as Banksy self-destructed a few seconds after being sold for $1.4 million at an auction.

99.
The Barrett M107 50-caliber long-range sniper rifle is a firearm made for modern war on terrorism. A US Marine called customer service during a firefight and complained his weapon malfunctioned. The helpline advised him how to fire it again.

100.
Only two national capitals are named after a US President: Washington, D.C., and Monrovia, Liberia.

101.

Soyuz 21 was a 1976 Soviet manned mission to the *Salyut 5* space station. It was intended to last more than two months but ended after forty-nine days in orbit as the two cosmonauts complained about the insupportable bad odour in the space station.

102.

A modern Formula One car is capable of developing 3.5 g-force – which is three and a half times its weight – thanks to the aerodynamic downforce of its spoilers. That means, theoretically, at high speeds, they could drive upside down on the ceiling of a tunnel.

103.

Albert Hofmann was a Swiss scientist best known for being the first person to synthesise, ingest, and learn of the psychedelic effects of *lysergic acid diethylamide* (LSD). He lived up to 102.

104.

The town of Bekoji, in the highlands of Ethiopia (population 17,000), has among its citizens long-distance runners who have won sixteen Olympic medals in twenty years. The runners from this tiny town have won more gold medals than India in all Summer Olympic categories put together.

105.

Alexander I of Yugoslavia did not like Tuesdays as he had lost three of his loved ones on this day. He became very superstitious and refused to take audiences or to go out to the public on a Tuesday. He was assassinated on 9 October 1934, a Tuesday.

106.

Panama is the only country where the sun can rise from the Pacific Ocean and set into the Atlantic Ocean (due to Panama's specific shape).

107.

In Russia, bears were observed on multiple occasions to get high by sniffing discarded aviation fuel barrels.

108.

Turkey granted voting rights to women fifteen years ahead of France.

109.

The world's closest international airports are Eilat, Israel, and Aqaba, Jordan, with a distance of only 6 km between them (4 mi). To make it even more crowded, the international airport of a third country (Taba, Egypt) is just 18 km (11 mi) away from Eilat.

110.

In 2001, a study by Danner, Snowdon, and Friesen found a relationship between being happy and living longer. They looked closely at autobiographies 180 Catholic nuns wrote at an average age of 22. The relation between emotional content and survival was assessed at age 75–94. Nuns writing more positive autobiographies when entering the convent in young adulthood lived longer than nuns writing less positive autobiographies.

111.

In December 2018, Russian state television showed a hi-tech humanoid robot. It turned out to be simply a man in a suit.

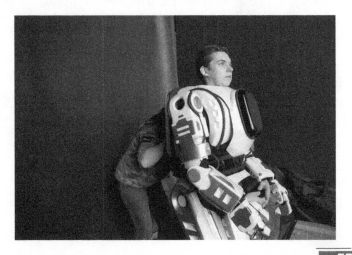

112.

Colombia is the country that mines and produces the most emeralds for the global market.

113.

Venezuela is the first and only country to win the four global pageants (Miss World, Miss Universe, Miss International, and Miss Earth) multiple times.

114.

The Siachen Glacier, Kashmir, is the highest battleground on Earth, where India and Pakistan have fought intermittently between 1984 and 2003. Both countries maintain a permanent military presence in the region at the height of over 6,000 metres (20,000 ft). There are the world's highest helipad, permanently manned post, and telephone booth.

115.

In late 2018, Google's CEO explained to the US Congress why a picture of Donald Trump comes up when you search for "idiot".

116.

In Chinese, you always list directions in a clockwise manner: East, South, West, North.

117.

When the Chinese invented gunpowder in the 9th century, they were trying to develop the alchemical formula of immortality.

118.

A baboon called Jackie served in the 3rd South African Infantry Regiment during World War I. He saluted superior officers, stood sentry, and was even wounded by enemy fire. For his bravery, Jackie was awarded a medal for valour, as well as promoted from private to corporal.

JACKIE   Mascot of the 3RD STH AFRICAN INF.

119.

In 1972, French physicist, Francis Perrin, made a discovery in the Oklo region of Gabon: in the past, several self-sustaining nuclear chain reactions had occurred, averaging probably less than 100 kW of thermal power over the course of hundreds of thousands of years.

120.

The "Cornfield Bomber" was the nickname given to a US Air Force F-106. In 1970, during a training exercise, it made an unpiloted landing in a farmer's field in Montana, USA, suffering only minor damage, after the pilot had ejected from the aircraft. The aircraft, recovered and repaired,
was returned to service.

121.

On 4 July 1989, a pilotless MiG-23 jet fighter of the Soviet Air Forces crashed into a house in Kortrijk, Belgium, killing one person. The pilot had ejected over an hour earlier in Poland due to technical problems, but the aircraft continued flying for around 900 km (600 mi) before running out of fuel and falling to the ground. The unmanned aircraft crossed the airspace of five countries: Poland, East Germany, West Germany, the Netherlands, and Belgium.

122.

"Grand Theft Auto V" is the highest-grossing video game as of writing. It has made over 6 billion dollars, more than twice as much as the highest-grossing movie, "Avengers: Endgame".

123.

In late 2018, a tank in Westönnen, Germany, leaked about a tonne of liquid chocolate into the street. The chocolate quickly solidified and effectively closed the road for a day.

124.

Up until 1919, the present Slovak capital, Bratislava, was mostly known in English by its German name, *Pressburg*, since after 1526 it was primarily dominated by the Habsburg Monarchy, and the city had a relevant ethnic-German population.

125.

In 1807, a rabbit hunt organised for the French Emperor, Napoleon Bonaparte, went wrong when several thousand tame rabbits were released in a field. Unlike wild hares, they were not afraid of people and came in packs towards Napoleon and company. The famous commander had to retreat.

126.

In Sudan, they get high on giraffe's liver. A drink called "umm nyolokh" is made from the bone marrow and liver of giraffes, and is said to contain the psychedelic chemical DMT.

127.

The tallest chocolate Easter egg measured over 10 m (34 ft) in height and was exhibited at Le Acciaierie Shopping Centre, in Cortenuova, Italy, on 16 April 2011. It weighed 7,200 kg (15,873 pounds) and had a circumference of almost 20 m (64 ft) at its widest point.

128.

Every month, we produce more steel than all the gold ever extracted throughout human history.

129.

1276 was one of the most turbulent years for the Roman Catholic Church: four Popes changed.

130.

The Four Great Inventions from ancient China are celebrated in Chinese culture for their historical significance: the compass, the printing, the papermaking, and the gunpowder.

131.

Jan Zizka was a Czech general and the most successful Hussite military leader (1360-1424). He amassed a number of victories and, shortly before he died of the plague, he wished for his skin to be made into drums so he could forever lead his troops into battle. His army extensively used gunpowder weapons and the English words *pistol* and *howitzer* derived from the Czech ones *pistala* and *houfnice* respectively.

132.

The phobia of palindromes is called *aibohphobia*, which is itself a palindrome.

133.

James Naismith, who invented the game of basketball, was the first basketball coach of the University of Kansas, USA. He remains the only coach in the university's history with a losing record.

134.

In 1409, amidst the period known as the *Great Schism*, or *Western Schism*, there were three Popes. Benedict XIII reigned in Avignon, France, Gregory XII reigned in Rome, Italy, and Alexander V succeeded by John XXIII reigned in Pisa, Italy.

135.

The English writer, Herbert George Wells, described World War I as "The war to end all wars".

136.

Maximilien Robespierre, arguably the best-known figure in the French revolution, was very enthusiastic about the guillotine and sent thousands of people to die on the guillotine. Eventually, he also ended up guillotined.

137.

In Muslim countries, people are more generous to beggars and charities at times of prayer.

138.
Gokulnath Shetty systemically defrauded the Punjab National Bank (India) for a total of nearly $1.8 billion over six years, and no-one noticed until early 2018.

139.
Since early 2019, commuters who use one of the most crowded subway lines outside morning peak hours in Tokyo, Japan, are being rewarded with free noodles.

140.
In July 2018, the UK government announced plans to install in-cell phones in 20 prisons in England and Wales to tackle the flow of illegal mobiles and reduce tension in wings.

141.
In 2016, Norway became the first country to stop cutting down trees, a huge step toward curbing global deforestation.

142.
In 2018, Algeria banned the imports of 851 products (including cars) in a bid to ease financial pressure caused by lower oil and gas revenue. In early 2019, it lifted the ban of many of those, but importing cars is still prohibited.

143.

A picture of an egg has over 53 million likes on Instagram.

144.

The intervals between two years of the same calendar type is always 6, 11, 12, 28, or 40 years. That means you can reuse that beautiful wall calendar again if you wait at least six years and at most forty.

145.

The American Civil War ended in 1865, but the US government was paying a veteran's pension from that conflict in 2017. Irene Triplett – the then 87-year-old daughter of a Civil War veteran – still collected part of her father's military pension. The last Civil War widow, Irene's mother, died in 2008 at the age of 93. The last surviving Civil War veteran died in 1956 at the age of 109.

146.

A cheetah can accelerate faster than a Lamborghini Gallardo from 0 to 100 km/h (0-62 mph). The predator does this in just three seconds and needs only three to four strides.

147.

Wardrobing is buying an item of clothing, wearing it for a while without removing the tag, and then returning it in such a state that the store has to accept it but cannot resell it. The US clothing industry estimates annual losses to 16 billion dollars.

148.

Warner Bros. was founded before the fall of the Ottoman Empire. Warner Bros. Studios was established in 1918, while the Ottoman Empire collapsed in 1922 when the last sultan was forced to step down.

149.

Vanessa Williams's parents announced her birth with "future miss USA". She won the title in 1984. Later in the same year, she gave up her title over a scandal involving nude photos. She was the first black Miss America and the first to give up the title.

150.

The *okapi*, also known as the forest giraffe, Congolese giraffe, or zebra giraffe, is a mammal native to the northeast of the Democratic Republic of the Congo in Central Africa. Although the okapi has striped markings reminiscent of zebras, it is most closely related to the giraffe. It remained unknown to the Western world until the 20th century.

151.

In early 2019, cotton seeds on China's lunar probe *Chang'e-4* sprouted, becoming the first plants to ever germinate on the Moon. The seeds are part of a biosphere experiment on the lander, to help prepare for future human settlements.

152.

"Tora! Tora! Tora!" was the code-phrase Japanese military used to inform their HQ about the success of the Pearl Harbor surprise attack. "Tora" is Japanese for "tiger".

153.

Toilet paper appeared on the Soviet market in the late 1960s, after the USSR had sent a man to space.

154.

In January 2019, an autonomous robot was struck and "killed" by a self-driving Tesla S in Las Vegas, USA.

155.

The older you are, the higher the chances of sharing fake news on social media.

156.

In 1665, when Isaac Newton first passed white light through a prism and watched it fan out into a rainbow, he identified seven constituent colours – red, orange, yellow, green, blue, indigo, and violet – not necessarily because that is how many hues he saw, but because he thought that the colours of the rainbow were analogous to the notes of the musical scale.

157.

In 2004, the Lexington Herald-Leader newspaper in Kentucky, USA, issued a front-page apology for "failing to cover the civil rights movement adequately four decades earlier".

158.

Luxembourg's ninth sovereign, Grand Duke Jean, died aged 98 in April 2019. At that time, he was the world's oldest living monarch and the only head of state to have participated in the D-Day Battle in 1944.

159.

Augustus James Pleasonton (1808-1894) was a militia general during the American Civil War. He wrote the pseudo-scientific book "The Influence of the Blue Ray of the Sunlight and of the Blue Color of the Sky", which was published in 1876. His theory led to what was called the "Blue-glass Craze", whereby people began growing crops under blue light. Soon, blue panes of glass were being sold as a way to increase crop production.

160.

The shortest Russian border is with North Korea: just 17 km (11 mi).

161.

If we count exclaves, Morocco and Spain share the shortest state border of just 85 m (280 ft), separating Morocco from Spain's outpost of
Peñón de Vélez de la Gomera.

162.

Zambia and Botswana share a border of only 150 m. By the way, this border is equal to the distance between Namibia and Zimbabwe, which do not share a border but are really close to each other.

163.

In early 2019, authorities in the northern Chinese province of Hebei released an app that can tell people if they are walking near someone in debt.

164.

Winterval was a season of public events in Birmingham, England, organised by Birmingham City Council in the winter periods of 1997-98 and 1998-99. The intention was to encourage people into the refurbished city centre with secular and religious events during the relevant period. The name "Winterval" has since been used in the UK as shorthand for "political correctness gone mad".

165.

In 1990, a container ship spilt thousands of Nike shoes off the coast of Alaska, USA, which helped oceanographers further understand ocean currents and is referred to as the "Great Shoe Spill of 1990".

166.

The word "bayonet" means "from Bayonne", the name of a town in southwest France, where they were made first.

167.

In 2018, Tunisia became the first Arab country to approve gender equality in inheritance law. The controversial law permits women and men to have an equal inheritance, contradicting the Qur'anic verse which states the share of women's inheritance is half that of men's.

168.

Chindōgu is a prank originating from Japan, which is done by a person seemingly inventing ingenious everyday gadgets that seem like an ideal solution to a particular problem, but are in fact nothing more than a useless gag. Ironically, the selfie stick, featured in a 1995 book of "101 Useless Japanese Inventions", later gained global popularity in the 21st century.

169.

Terrance Stanley "Terry" Fox (1958-1981) was a Canadian athlete, humanitarian, and cancer research activist. In 1980, with one leg amputated due to cancer, he embarked on an east-to-west cross-Canada run to raise money and awareness for cancer research. Although the spread of his cancer eventually forced him to end his quest after 143 days and 5,373 kilometres (3,339 mi), and ultimately cost him his life, his efforts resulted in a lasting, worldwide legacy.

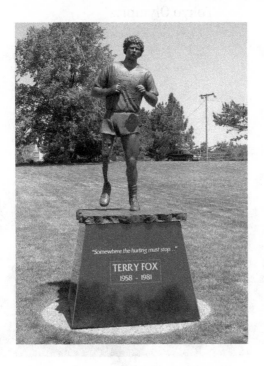

170.
In 2018, a newly discovered blind and burrowing amphibian was officially named *Dermophis donaldtrumpi*, in recognition of the US President's climate change denial.

171.
The *Shinkansen*, known in English as the bullet train, is a network of high-speed railway lines in Japan. It began service on 1 October 1964, in time for the first Tokyo Olympics.

172.

Ireland is one of the few countries where windmills turn clockwise.

173.

In the decades before the 9/11 attacks, Peru and El Salvador were in the top 3 countries by a number of terrorist attacks. Now, neither of them make it into the top 10.

174.

In 2018, the world's oldest spider on record died in Australia at the age of 43.

175.

The Kettle War was a military confrontation between the troops of the Holy Roman Empire and the Republic of the Seven Netherlands on 8 October 1784. The only shot fired hit a soup kettle, hence the name.

176.

Scientists discovered *Turritopsis dohrnii* back in 1883, and only recently did they find out it was technically capable of living forever. When faced with stressors like starvation or injury, the jellyfish reverts to its youngest form, a cyst that is genetically identical to the original.

177.

Flamingos, ravens, and parrots in captivity can live longer than humans.

178.

Since 2016, there has been a Minister of State for Happiness in the United Arab Emirates Cabinet. The responsibility is to "align and drive government policy to create social good and satisfaction".

179.

The notorious Roman Emperor Caligula stopped a planned attack on Britain and suddenly declared war on the sea god Neptune. He made two Roman legions collect seashells and attack ocean waves.

180.

Raccoons were scavenging the recycle bins in Toronto, Canada, and the city authorities invested money and efforts to create "raccoon-resistant" bins. Soon after the rollout of the new bins, the raccoons learned how to open them.

181.

Unlike old dogs, old adults can indeed learn new tricks thanks to a protein molecule called *netrin*.

182.

In 1995, Foutanga Babani Sissoko convinced an employee of the Dubai Islamic Bank that he knew "black magic" that allowed him to "double any amount he has in his possession". Long story short, the naïve employee transferred him the equivalent of 242 million US dollars over the course of three years.

183.

Whisky can be made from diabetics' urine as it contains sugar.

184.

The US Census Bureau removed the category "Central or South American" from the census because many people from the Midwest and the South would mistakenly pick it.

185.

Carlos Henrique Raposo (born 2 April 1963), aka Carlos Kaiser, is a Brazilian former football player, better known as being a "farce footballer". He was selected to play with many teams during his decade-long career, but never actually played a regulation game and hid his limited ability with injuries, frequent team changes and other ruses.

186.

In Myanmar, people use the words "internet" and "Facebook" interchangeably.

187.

The weed *qat* is Yemen's most popular drug: 90% of men and over a third of women habitually chew its leaves, storing the masticated greenery in their cheek until the narcotic seeps into their bloodstream.

188.

Christ the King is the tallest statue of Jesus in the world (33 m or 108 ft). Located in Swiebodzin, Poland, it broadcasts wireless internet to the surrounding villages.

189.

Recent *grolar* or *pizzly* bear occurrences have been the result of a male grizzly mating with a female polar bear. Male grizzlies can travel long distances looking for a mate while female grizzly bears tend to stay farther south.

190.

In 2018, Domino's Pizza in Russia was forced to end a marketing promotion that went viral, offering a lifetime of free pizza to fans who got the company's logo tattooed "in a prominent place", after too many people participated.

191.

The author of multiple books about how to not get gored by bulls, Bill Hillmann, was the only non-Spaniard to get gored in the 2014 running of the bulls in Pamplona, Spain.

192.

The small mountain town of Rattenberg, Austria, barely sees any sun during the winter. But with the aid of a few mirrors, its inhabitants enjoy the sunshine again. Thirty heliostats, permanently rotating mirrors, mounted on a hillside now grab sunshine off reflectors from the neighbouring village of Kramsach.

193.

A small town in the US state of Missouri is stirring controversy after announcing the title of its new local newspaper, the "Uranus Examiner".

194.

Mark Pollock (born in 1976) was the first blind person to race to the South Pole and has also won silver and bronze medals for rowing at the Commonwealth Games.

195.

In certain parts of Nigeria, "rainmakers" are held in high regard and paid to keep the rain away from events.

196.

According to a 2015 Australian study, the accuracy of the most popular smartphone apps for weight loss is "suboptimal" and their indication cannot be trusted.

197.

During the Korean War, the Soviet Union saw the chance of disposing of vast numbers of arms seized during WWII from Nazi Germany to North Korea. Therefore, many of the soldiers of the North were using the notorious MP 40, aka *Schmeisser*.

198.

The *Blue Banana* (also known as the *European Megalopolis* or the *Manchester-Milan Axis*) is a discontinuous corridor of urbanisation spreading over Western and Central Europe with a population of around 111 million people.

199.

In 2018, the minister in charge of Japan's cybersecurity, Yoshitaka Sakurada, said he had never used a computer.

200.

"The 85 Ways to Tie a Tie" is a book by Thomas Fink and Yong Mao. The authors were research fellows at Cambridge University's Cavendish Laboratory. It was first published in 1999 and subsequently translated into nine other languages.

201.

On Canadian radio, you are allowed to say the f-word during the daytime if you are speaking French, but not if you are speaking English. *Au Canada, on a le droit de dire fuck à la radio dans une émission francophone. Par contre, c'est interdit dans les émissions en anglais.*

202.

Since 1997, there has been a tiny, self-declared Republic of Užupis located inside the Lithuanian capital of Vilnius. Its constitution states among others that "Everyone has the right to be happy" and "Everyone has the right to be unhappy".

203.

In 2018, drunk birds were causing havoc in the town of Gilbert, Minnesota, USA. The local Police Department received multiple reports of birds that appeared to be "under the influence", flying into windows and cars, and acting confused. They got intoxicated by eating fermented berries.

204.

In 1969, a ceramic plate containing the artworks of six prominent artists from the late 1960s (Warhol, Rauschenberg, Novros, Myers, Oldenburg, and Chamberlain) was carried on Apollo 12 and left on the Moon. One of the pictures on it is a dick pic.

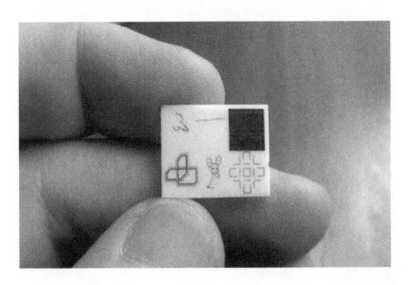

205.

In 2018, a woman was charged with theft in Taiwan for stealing a yoghurt drink (value below two dollars) from her roommate after being identified by a DNA test. The investigation cost Taiwanese taxpayers about 500 euro (600 US dollars).

206.

Although the population of Indonesia is predominantly Muslim and Christian, 83% of the people on the touristic island of Bali identify as Hindu.

207.

People become more creative when they are in contact with other cultures.

208.

Gallium was the first chemical element to confirm Mendeleev's prediction of the periodic table.

209.

In the 1990s, Subway was involved in more legal disputes than any other fast-food chain, more than the combined total listed by its seven largest competitors (McDonald's, Burger King, KFC, Pizza Hut, Wendy's, Taco Bell, and Hardee's).

210.

The Bible forbids eating of chameleons.

211.

Thomas Edison invented the word "hello". Alexander Graham Bell initially used "ahoy" (as used on ships) as a telephone greeting.

212.

Now used for fitness, the treadmill was introduced initially in 1818 as a means of usefully occupying prison convicts in the UK.

213.

In 2013, male train drivers in Sweden requested permission to wear shorts in hot weather and were refused. They circumvented the ban on shorts by wearing skirts to work.

214.

According to the Guinness Book of World Records, the fastest clapper (as of 2018) clapped his hands 1,103 times in one minute. His name is Eli Bishop from the USA.

215.
Pakistan is an acronym for Punjab, Afghan (the North-West frontier region), Kashmir, Indus (some say it is for Islam) and Sind. The "Tan" is said to represent Baluchistan.

216.
In many countries, hairdressers, shop owners, and bartenders have to pay royalties for playing the radio.

217.
Silver is the best conductor of electricity.

218.
In 2017, a baby gender reveal sparked a weeklong wildfire in Arizona, USA. Dennis Dickey and his wife brought an explosive target out into a yellow grassland to announce the gender of their expected baby with a bang. The mini-explosion started a fire, which went on to burn 47,000 acres, and cost 8.2 million US dollars (about 7.5 million euro) for 800 firefighters to put out.

219.
The Republic of South Africa has a whopping eleven official languages.

220.

The metric system was developed in Paris, France, in the late 18th century to make trade easier and calculations simpler. In 1793, France sent Joseph Dombey to the USA to meet with the then Secretary of State, Thomas Jefferson, and to convince him to adopt the system. In his first State of the Union address, George Washington had called the need for a standard unit of measurement "an object of great importance" and Jefferson was appointed to make this happen. The metric system was then made up of two standards of measurement – a rod that measured one meter and a copper cylinder that weighed one kilogram. Dombey travelled with both items but his ship was hit by a storm and he ended up in the Caribbean where pirates captured him. By the time France sent someone else to the USA, Edmond Randolph had become Secretary of the State and he did not really care about what measurements were used.

221.

Rob Furlong (born 1976) is a former Canadian military sniper who at one time held the record for the longest confirmed sniper kill in combat, at 2,430 m (2,657 yds). In 2009, his record was beaten by Craig Harrison (British Army), who shot two Taliban fighters at 2,475 m (2,707 yds).

222.

In World War II, the three most successful Soviet snipers had more than 1,500 kills combined: Mihail Surkov killed 702 enemy troops, Vasilij Kvachantiradze – 534 and Semen Nomokonov – 367.

223.

Casual Friday had its origin from Hawaii's custom of *Aloha Friday*. The latter slowly spread east to California, continuing around the globe until the 1990s when it became known as Casual Friday.

224.

Japan has an increasing number of vacant homes – a problem that is set to persist because of an ageing and shrinking population that has left many towns and villages empty. The phenomenon is called "akiya" and dedicated websites are promoting a growing number of vacant residential properties, many of which are being given away for free, with the buyer having to pay only taxes and fees such as agent commissions.

225.

Gabrielle Bonheur "Coco" Chanel (1883-1971) was a French fashion designer and businesswoman, the founder of the Chanel brand. She acted as a Nazi agent during the Second World War, carrying out several spy and recruitment missions.

226.

Mocha is a city in Yemen. The famous mokka coffee and desserts were named after it.

227.

The world's first practical submarine was built in 1620 by Dutch engineer, Cornelis Jacobszoon Drebbel, under the patronage of James I of England.

228.

In early 2019, the Lufthansa German Airlines sued a passenger for missing a flight. What is known as "skiplagging" flights is when a passenger looking to fly from "A" to "B" finds it cheaper to book a flight from "A" to "C" which stops at "B" en route to "C". The passenger exited when the aircraft stopped at "B".

229.

Shangri-La is a fictional place described in the 1933 novel "Lost Horizon" by British author James Hilton. Hilton describes Shangri-La as a mystical, harmonious valley, gently guided from a lamasery, enclosed in the western end of the Kunlun Mountains. It has become synonymous with any earthly paradise, particularly a mythical Himalayan utopia – a permanently happy land isolated from the world. In modern China, Zhongdian county was renamed *Xiānggélǐlā* (Shangri-La in Chinese) in 2001 to attract tourists.

230.

The film "Tron" (1982) was not considered for a Best Visual Effects Oscar award because the Academy at the time believed that using computers was cheating.

231.

Gerald Cotton, CEO of Cryptocurrency *QuadrigaCX* (Canada's largest cryptocurrency exchange), died in late 2018 in India. The unexpected death left 175 million euros (190 million US dollars) of cryptocurrency missing, supposedly locked in digital wallets to which only he had the password. Investigators, however, found only empty wallets and what had happened with the missing money is still a mystery. In April 2019, QuadrigaCX entered bankruptcy.

232.

In 1950, the US police in Miami, Florida, accidentally discovered a crime ring that had been stealing thousands of dollars from the local phone company for years. The thieves were young women employed in the counting room of the Southern Bell Telephone Company. They were smuggling money out of the building by hiding coin rolls in their bras. The case was dubbed "the case of the clinking brassieres", "the bra bandits", and "brassiere brigade".

233.

Ukrainians have a special attitude towards Star Wars characters. In 2014, a candidate named Darth Vader ran for president in Ukraine, while two men named Darth Vader were candidates at the Kiev mayoral election and the Odessa mayoral election. Candidates named Darth Vader reappeared in the 2015 Ukrainian local elections.

234.

Robert Smalls was born in 1839 into slavery on a South Carolina plantation. By the time the US Civil War came around, Smalls had become an experienced seaman, so he was assigned to steer a Confederate Navy vessel called the *Planter*, based out of Charleston. The crew consisted of a few white officers and several slaves. He managed to escape with all the slaves, their families, and the ship itself to the North. He then entered service in the Union Navy as a pilot on several vessels, including the repurposed Planter. In this role, he removed mines that he had helped lay as a slave and participated in a number of sea battles. Because of his bravery, Smalls was promoted to captain himself, becoming one of the highest-ranking and highest-paid black officers in the Civil War. Smalls leveraged his resulting fame into social activism, throwing his support into an initiative to educate former slaves, and becoming literate himself (in most Confederate states, it was illegal to teach a black person to read). He entered politics, serving in the South Carolina legislature before becoming one of the first black people elected to the US House of Representatives in 1874.

235.

Both "The Guiding Light" and "The Simpsons" TV series have a Springfield as a hometown.

236.

So far, there have been two astronauts named Aleksander Aleksandrov, from two different countries: USSR (performed two missions in 1983 and 1987) and Bulgaria (1988).

237.

Australian feral camels number about 300,000. The government is trying to limit their number by culling (shooting) them from helicopters and exporting live animals and meat to Saudi Arabia, the United Arab Emirates, Brunei, and Malaysia.

238.

In Australia, feral goats are often shot from helicopters. Another, more ingenious technique is the so-called *Judas goat*, which utilises radio-tracking equipment to locate herds of feral goats.

A captured goat, or "Judas", will be fitted with a collar, to which a radio transmitter is attached. Goats are a strongly social species and, within a few days, the Judas goat will join up with a herd of feral goats. This group can be located with the radio-tracking equipment and shot by hunters, either on foot or from helicopters.

239.

Native to South America, cane toads were introduced to Australia in 1935 in an attempt to control the native grey-backed cane beetle and French's beetle. These beetles are native to Australia and damage sugar cane crops. Since their release, toads have rapidly multiplied in population and now number over 200 million, and have been known to spread diseases affecting local biodiversity. And, by the way, they have not solved the problem with the beetles.

240.

In 1969, the former US President, Jimmy Carter (then Georgia governor and future POTUS), saw and reported a UFO.

241.

As of March 2019, three patients worldwide have become HIV-free after a bone marrow transplant.

242.

NASCAR (stock car racing) in the United States got its origins in bootlegging during the Prohibition in the USA (1919-1933). Bootleggers needed to distribute their illicit products, and they typically used small, fast vehicles to evade the police better.

243.

There is an abandoned town of mini castles in Turkey. The *Burj Al Babas* complex in the rolling hills of central Turkey is currently deserted. It was supposed to become a luxury residential retreat for the wealthy, made up of 732 copycat homes and a shopping centre. But works stopped in late 2018 when its developer, Sarot Group, filed for bankruptcy.

244.

Yellow margarine was banned in Wisconsin, USA, until 1967. Today, Wisconsin still has some margarine laws. Restaurants cannot legally serve margarine unless they also offer butter. Schools and prisons must serve butter to students and inmates, unless a doctor provides a valid health reason.

245.

The smallest surviving baby was born in Germany, in 2015, and weighed 252 g (slightly more than a half-pound).

246.

To qualify as a sword swallower, according to the Sword Swallowers' Association International, you need to swallow "a non-retractable, solid steel blade at least two centimetres wide and 38 centimetres long".

247.

It takes around three years of continuous use for a reusable cup to offset the ecological footprint of producing it, and more importantly, washing it in comparison with single-use cups.

248.

In 2007, in Badalona, Spain, a drug dealer decided to advertise his business. He distributed photocopies of a handwritten ad, containing (along with many typos) his name and address. The local police thought at the beginning that it was a joke as "no-one is that stupid", but eventually had to accept they were wrong and arrested the guy.

249.

The athletes from Taiwan compete at the Olympics under the name of a make-believe country: *Chinese Taipei*. Historically, before becoming fully independent, many countries participated in the Olympic Games under a different name, sometimes totally different from the present one. Some examples:

British Guiana: Prior to Guyana's independence in 1966, the country participated under the name British Guiana from 1948 to 1964.

British Honduras: Belize participated under its former name of British Honduras in 1968 and 1972.

Burma: Myanmar was known as Burma between 1948 and 1988.

Ceylon: Sri Lanka was known as Ceylon between 1948 and 1972.

Congo Kinshasa: The Democratic Republic of the Congo was known as Congo Kinshasa in 1968.

Dahomey: Benin was known as Dahomey in 1972.

Gold Coast: Before Ghana's independence in 1957, it participated in the 1952 Games as a British colony called the Gold Coast.

Ivory Coast: Côte d'Ivoire was known as Ivory Coast between 1964 and 1988.

Northern Rhodesia: Zambia achieved independence on the last day of the 1964 Games, but had participated as Northern Rhodesia during those Games.

Rhodesia: Southern Rhodesia (known as Zimbabwe since 1980) participated under the name of Rhodesia in 1928, 1960, and 1964.

Tanganyika: Although Tanganyika and Zanzibar had merged to form Tanzania before the 1964 Olympics, at their first Games, they competed under the name of Tanganyika.

United Arab Republic: Egypt participated as the United Arab Republic in 1964 and 1968. In 1960, they also competed under that name, but in a combined team with Syria.

Upper Volta: Burkina Faso was known as Upper Volta in 1972.

Zaire: The Democratic Republic of the Congo was known as Zaire between 1984 and 1996.

250.

The *Burj Khalifa* is a skyscraper in Dubai, United Arab Emirates. With a total height of 829.8 m (2,722 ft), it has been the tallest structure and building in the world since its inauguration in 2010. Originally called Burj Dubai, it was renamed Burj Khalifa in a tribute to Sheik Khalifa bin Zayed al-Nahayan, head of the United Arab Emirates and Ruler of Abu Dhabi, for lending Dubai money to pay its debts.

251.

In Singapore, the methodology to calculate ministerial salaries takes into account Singapore's economic performance; the real median income growth rate, real growth rate of lowest 20th percentile income, unemployment rate, and real GDP growth rate.

252.

Singapore has the longest automated metro system in the world with 82 km (51 mi).

253.

In 1985, Myanmar (then-Burma) government decided that money introduced in 1964 was not valid anymore. Denominations of 20, 50, and 100 kyats were declared to no longer be a legal tender, with a laughably low maximum amount for reimbursement: K5000. New notes – K25, K35, and K75 – were introduced in their place, only to be taken out two years later, this time with compensation of just K100 allowed for trade-in, allegedly to let students return home from school.

254.

A star racing pigeon named Armando was sold for a record 1.25 million euro (1.5 million dollars) in an online auction in Belgium. A Chinese buyer acquired the prized bird.

255.

Aristides de Sousa Mendes do Amaral e Abranches (1885 – 1954) was a Portuguese consul in Bordeaux, France, during World War II. He defied the orders of António de Oliveira Salazar's Estado Novo regime, issuing visas and passports to some 30,000 refugees fleeing Nazi Germany, including Jews. For this, Sousa Mendes was punished by the Salazar regime but was eventually vindicated in 1988, more than a decade after the Carnation Revolution, which toppled the Estado Novo.

256.

The union between the kingdoms of Norway and Sweden lasted 91 years (1814-1905). Its dissolution led to Sweden's recognition of Norway as an independent constitutional monarchy on 26 October 1905.

257.

People with lighter eyes tend to be more sensitive to light, a result of having less pigment in the iris to protect them from sunlight. This can place them at a greater risk of macular degeneration and other eye-related problems.

258.

Andorra could be considered a semi-elective principality. Andorra's two heads of state are Spain's Bishop of La Seu d'Urgell and, since 1589, the king of France. As the French monarchy has long since been eliminated, the position of co-prince of Andorra falls to the democratically elected President of France. However, the Andorran authorities or people have no say in the election of the President of France, leaving Andorra in the unique position of having a monarch who is democratically elected by the citizenry of another state.

259.

Delivery trucks of the company UPS avoid making left-hand turns. This seemingly silly strategy started in the 1970s and has paid off: UPS's routing software shaved 20.4 million miles off their routes in 2016 while delivering 350,000 more packages. It also diminished CO_2 emissions by 20,000 metric tons.

260.

Making a left turn at a US crossroad is three times more likely to kill pedestrians than turning right.

261.

Alexander the Great is known as *Iskander* in the Muslim world.

262.

Clever Hans was a horse that was claimed to have performed arithmetic and other intellectual tasks in Germany. After a formal investigation in 1907, psychologist Oskar Pfungst demonstrated that the horse was not actually performing these mental tasks, but was watching the reactions of his trainer. He discovered that the horse was responding directly to involuntary cues in the body language of the human trainer, who was solving the problem.

263.

Nansen passports, originally and officially stateless persons' passports, were internationally recognised refugee travel documents from 1922 to 1938. They were first issued by the League of Nations to stateless refugees. They quickly became known as "Nansen passports" for their promoter, the Norwegian statesman and polar explorer, Fridtjof Nansen.

264.

In the 1820s, Louis Spohr introduced the conductor's baton. A *baton*, which is the French word for "stick", is used by conductors primarily to enlarge and enhance the manual and bodily movements associated with directing an ensemble of musicians. Prior to its invention, conductors would often use a violin bow.

265.

More than 90% of the living creatures weighing over 5 kg (11 pounds) are either humans or domesticated animals.

266.

The global grey wolf population is estimated to be 300,000. The global dog population is estimated to be at 900 million: 3,000 times as numerous.

267.

Unlike the soldiers on the Western Front during WWI, the vast majority of Russian soldiers were never issued metal helmets.

268.

Draculin (named after Count Dracula) is a glycoprotein found in the saliva of vampire bats. It acts as a strong anticoagulant, thus keeping the blood of the bitten victim from clotting while the bat is drinking.

269.

Saudi Arabia is the largest producer of desalinated water in the world. Desalination plants provide about half the country's drinking water.

270.

In 1951, a German soldier was found alive after being trapped with five comrades following the dynamiting of their underground storehouse in 1945 at the very end of World War II. They were in a storehouse in Babie Doly, Poland, when retreating soldiers blew up the tunnel unaware that there were people inside. The stores contained a large amount of food, drink, candles, and other goods, so the soldiers were able to survive. Four of the soldiers died (two suicides soon after being trapped, and two unknown causes), leaving only two survivors. One of them suffered a heart attack and died upon leaving the tunnel. The final soldier was said to have made a full recovery, but his identity was never revealed.

271.

In 2017, researchers from the British energy price comparison platform, Power Compare, discovered that the total volume of electricity required for mining Bitcoin – the computational process that keeps transactions on the blockchain moving – amounted to more consumption than 159 individual countries. Among others, the list includes European countries such as Ireland, Croatia, Serbia, Slovakia, Iceland, and almost all African countries.

272.

The *Sheikh Zayed Mosque* in Abu Dhabi is unique with some of its features. The mosque is the largest in the UAE and the third-largest in the world. It has the largest single piece of hand-made carpet worldwide. Using 38 tons of cotton and wool, 1,200 weavers from Iran's Khorasan Province crafted the rug over the period of a year and a half. The finished product incorporates 2.2 billion individual, hand-tied knots, covers 5,627 m² (60,570 sq ft), and weighs 12 tons. The courtyard, with its floral design, measures about 17,000 m² (180,000 sq ft) and is considered to be the largest example of marble mosaic in the world. The seven chandeliers incorporate millions of Swarovski crystals. The largest of them is the second-largest known chandelier inside a mosque, with a diameter of 10 m (33 ft) and a height of 15 m (49 ft).

273.

Belgian inventor and musician, Adolphe Sax, invented the saxophone and presented to the world for the first time at the 1841 Brussels Exhibition.

274.

The *Indiana Pi Bill* is the popular name for bill #246 of the 1897 sitting of the Indiana General Assembly, USA, one of the most notorious attempts to establish mathematical truth by legislative fiat. Despite its name, the main result claimed by the bill is a method to square the circle, rather than to establish a specific value for the mathematical constant π, the ratio of the circumference of a circle to its diameter. The bill, written by an amateur mathematician, Edward J. Goodwin, does imply various incorrect values of π, such as 3.2. The bill never became law due to the intervention of Professor C. A. Waldo of Purdue University, who happened to be present in the legislature on the day it went up for a vote.

275.

Mary Ann Franco (from Florida, USA) gradually became blind after injuring her spine in a car accident in 1993. In 2015, she fell at home injuring her spine again and, after an operation, regained sight after 20 years of blindness.

276.

The global average fertility rate is just below
2.5 children per woman (as of 2019). Over the last
50 years, the global fertility rate has halved. In Iran,
for example, the fertility rate in 1985 was 6.2 children
per woman; today, women in Iran have fewer children
than in the US, the UK, or Sweden: 1.7 children
per woman.

277.

Conflict Kitchen is a restaurant in Pittsburgh, USA,
that serves cuisine from countries with which the
United States is in conflict.

278.

The Underground City is a Cold War-era bomb shelter
consisting of a network of tunnels located beneath
Beijing, China. The government claimed that the
tunnels could accommodate all of Beijing's six million
inhabitants. It covers an area of 85 square kilometres
(33 sq mi), 8 to 18 metres (26-59 ft) under
the surface.

279.

Cockroaches deploy a stunning, and largely unstudied,
karate-style kick to prevent wasp attacks that would
turn the cockroaches into "zombies".

280.

The world's largest statue, the Statue of Unity, in Gujarat, India, was inaugurated in 2018. At 182 m tall or 240 m including the base (597 ft and 787 ft respectively), it is twice the height of the US Statue of Liberty and depicts India's first deputy Prime Minister, Sardar Vallabhbhai Patel.

281.

The largest recognised chandelier in the world hangs inside the Sultan Qaboos Grand Mosque. The chandelier is located in Oman and weighs a phenomenal 8.5 tons.

282.

The largest snowflake ever recorded was 38 cm (15 in) wide. In 1887, a snowflake with such dimensions fell on the Fort Keogh Army Post in Montana, USA, and is still considered the largest ever.

283.

In late 1992, Coca-Cola released a product specifically designed to fail. It all started when Pepsi introduced *Crystal Pepsi* in early 1992. It was one of the most successful new soda product launches in history, with more than $470 million in sales in its first year. In response, Coca-Cola released a copycat product: *Tab Clear*. In a bid to confuse the consumers, Coke's beverage was branded deliberately as Tab – a sugar-free drink that had not been popular since the 1970s and which was sweetened with saccharine – which was linked forever with causing cancer in laboratory mice. Tab Clear did not sell well at all, but in 1993, Crystal Pepsi's sales plummeted, too. Both products were discontinued in the course of the following year.

284.

Wilma Glodean Rudolph (1940-1994) was an African-American sprinter who became a world-record-holding Olympic champion and international sports icon in track and field following her successes in the 1956 and 1960 Olympic Games. What makes these achievements even more remarkable is the fact that she contracted infantile paralysis (caused by the poliovirus) at the age of five and had to wear a leg brace until she was twelve years old.

285.

In 2018, the campaign of a sitting US president facing re-election opted to market its list for the first time ever. This means that Donald Trump's supporters list, containing 20 million names, emails, and phone numbers, is for sale.

286.

José Salvador Alvarenga is a Salvadoran fisherman and author who was found on 30 January 2014 on the Marshall Islands after spending 14 months adrift in a fishing boat in the Pacific Ocean, beginning on 17 November 2012. He survived on a diet of raw fish, turtles, small birds, sharks, and rainwater. He is the first person in recorded history to have survived in a small boat lost at sea for more than a year.

287.

Orgone is a pseudo-scientific spiritual concept variously described as an esoteric energy or hypothetical universal life force. Originally proposed in the 1930s by Wilhelm Reich and developed by Reich's student, Charles Kelley, after Reich's death in 1957, orgone was seen as a massless, omnipresent substance, similar to the luminiferous aether. It was more closely associated with living energy than with inert matter. Reich argued that deficits in bodily orgone were at the root of many diseases, much as deficits or constrictions in the libido could produce neuroses in Freudian theory. He designed special "orgone accumulators" – devices ostensibly for collecting and storing orgone energy from the environment – to improve general health or even to control the weather. Ultimately, the US Food and Drug Administration obtained a federal injunction barring the distribution of orgone-related materials, on the grounds that Reich and his associates were making false and misleading claims, and later jailed Reich and destroyed all orgone-related materials at the institute after Reich violated the injunction.

288.

In March 2019, a British Airways flight destined for Düsseldorf, Germany, landed in Edinburgh, Scotland, by mistake.

289.

The cathedral Notre-Dame de Paris is the 0 km for all national roads in France. In April 2019, it was badly damaged in a fire and its complete restoration could require up to twenty years. It is noteworthy that donations of over €1 billion were pledged for the cathedral's reconstruction within a couple of days after the calamity.

290.

Dumdum bullets received their name from Dum Dum, the town and arsenal in eastern India where such bullets were first produced.

291.

Ming the clam, the world's oldest animal, was killed in 2013 at the age of 507 years by scientists trying to determine its age. Known as Ming, the bivalve mollusc was 'born' in 1499, meaning it was swimming in the oceans before Henry VIII took the English throne. It was named after the Chinese Ming dynasty, which was in power when it was alive.

292.

In 2019, a senior member of the Italian far-right League party, Massimiliano Fedriga, who is an outspoken critic of Italy's mandatory vaccination rules was treated in hospital after contracting chickenpox.

293.

Operation Haudegen was the name of a German operation during the Second World War to establish meteorological stations on Svalbard, Norway, 1,050 km (650 mi) from the North Pole. The station was active from 9 September 1944 to 4 September 1945, when the German personnel were picked up by a Norwegian seal-hunting vessel and surrendered to its captain. The group of men were the last German troops to surrender after the Second World War.

294.

During the 2018-2019 regular season, players of NBA (National Basketball Association, USA) made 27,955 3-point shots. That is more than what they made during the entire decade of the 1980s (23,871).

295.

On 6 May 2010, *Flash Crash*, also known as the *Crash of 2:45* or the *2010 Flash Crash*, was a United States trillion-dollar stock market crash, which lasted for 36 minutes. Stock indices, such as the S&P 500, Dow Jones Industrial Average, and Nasdaq Composite collapsed and rebounded very rapidly. The Dow Jones Industrial Average had its second-biggest intraday point drop (from the opening) up to that point, plunging 998.5 points (about 9%), most within minutes, only to recover a large part of the loss. In 2015, the US Department of Justice laid "22 criminal counts, including fraud and market manipulation" against Navinder Singh Sarao, a trader.

296.

In Colombia, two pairs of identical twins (born in 1988) were mixed up after birth and grew up apart. They met by chance 25 years later in Bogota and learned the truth. Their case is a unique opportunity for research on identical twins and "nature vs nurture".

297.

Since 2018, a South Korean school has been enrolling illiterate grandmothers as it is running out of first graders. Presently, several women aged 56 to 80 are attending the school, sometimes alongside their grandchildren.

298.

The scaly-foot snail has evolved a shell made of iron sulphide. Bacteria seem to be synthesising the iron and building the armour. No other animal on Earth can use the iron this way. It lives around hydrothermal vents, where seawater percolates into the crust and is heated by underlying magma, reaching 400 °C (750 °F), pouring out, and bringing toxins with it.

299.

The US felon, Steven Russell, escaped prison by using laxatives to fake symptoms of AIDS. He then called the prison, posing as a doctor, asking for prisoners interested in experimental treatment and volunteered. Once out of Texas, he sent a death certificate to the prison stating he died.

300.

A study from 2011 confirmed that placebo-healing techniques are more efficient when accompanied by sophisticated rituals and drama.

301.

Yasser Arafat (1929-2004) was co-founder and Chairman of the Palestine Liberation Organization, President of the Palestinian National Authority, and co-recipient of the Nobel Peace Prize in 1994. When speaking at the United Nations General Assembly in 1974, he appeared wearing his gun belt and holster. He said in his speech: "Today, I have come bearing an olive branch and a freedom fighter's gun. Do not let the olive branch fall from my hand".

302.

In Singapore, some public elevators come equipped with *Urine Detection Devices* that set off an alarm and close the doors when any odour of urine is detected until the police arrive.

303.

Amazon Alexa, known simply as Alexa, is a virtual assistant developed by Amazon. "She" receives hundreds of marriage proposals every day.

304.

In 2019 (shortly before the presidential elections in June), the Kazakh police took a young activist into custody after he decided to test whether he could get away with standing in the street holding a placard with nothing written on it. Aslan Sagutdinov was standing with the placard in front of the central council offices of Oral when the police arrested him, only to release him a few hours later.

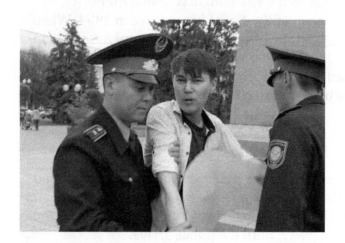

305.

Nur-sultan, previously Astana, is the capital city of Kazakhstan. On 23 March 2019, following a unanimous vote in Kazakhstan's parliament, the city was renamed Nur-Sultan, after former president Nursultan Nazarbayev.

306.

Spending on festivals is an essential part of the budget for many impoverished households. Low-income families around the world – those living on less than $2 a day – spend much of their income on goods that do not appear to alleviate poverty. For example, the average spending on festivals is as high as 15 percent of income in some regions of India. Similarly, South Africans spend, on average, a year's income on an adult's funeral, often financed by borrowing.

307.

Australia's latest A$50 note contains an embarrassing typo. The Reserve Bank of Australia spelt "responsibility" as "responsibilty" on 46 million of the new notes.

308.

The sovereign nation of Liberia is often described as "never colonised" because it was created so recently, in 1847, as a colony of American ex-slaves. Ethiopia is also considered "never colonised", despite Italy's occupation from 1936–1941 because this did not result in a lasting colonial administration. In the 1880s, Italy failed to take Abyssinia (as Ethiopia was then known) as a colony.

309.

Only two kings have so far won gold Olympic medals. In 1928, then Crown Prince Olav of Norway, a nephew of King George V of Great Britain, received a gold medal in the six-metre class yachting at the Amsterdam Olympics. King Constantine II of Greece received the gold medal in sailing (Dragon Class) at the 1960 Summer Olympics in Rome with his elder sister, Princess Sofia, the future Queen of Spain, serving as a reserve for the Greek team.

310.

The colour magenta was named after Magenta in northern Italy, site of a battle (1859) fought shortly before the red dye was discovered.

311.

In 2018, Swiss cheesemaker Beat Wampfler and a team of researchers from the Bern University of Arts exposed nine wheels of Emmental cheese to an endless, 24-hour loop of various types of music. The cheese was then examined by food technologists from the ZHAW Food Perception Research Group, who concluded that the cheese exposed to music had a milder flavour compared to the non-musical cheese. They also found that hip-hop cheese had a stronger aroma and stronger flavour than other samples, exposed to classical music, rock, or techno.

312.
The silhouette on the NBA (National Basketball Association of the USA) logo – a player dribbling and swivelling between a red and blue background – is LA Lakers' legend Jerry West.

313.
Haru Urara is a Japanese racehorse. The horse gained nationwide popularity in 2003, not due to her success, but rather due to a long string of consecutive losses. She has not yet officially retired but has not raced since September 2004. She currently maintains a record of 0 wins and 113 losses.

314.

Volodymyr Oleksandrovych Zelensky (born 1978) is a Ukrainian politician, screenwriter, actor, comedian, and director who is the 6th President of Ukraine since 20 May 2019. In a television series called Servant of the People (aired from 2015 to 2019), Zelensky played the role of President of Ukraine.

315.

You have probably heard of identical and fraternal twins, but a report published in early 2019 states there is a third kind: *sesquizygous* twins or "semi-identical". Identical or *monozygotic* twins develop from a single fertilised egg that eventually splits in two and forms two identical boys or two girls. They share 100% of their DNA. Fraternal or *dizygotic* twins form from two eggs that have been fertilised by two of the father's sperm, producing two genetically unique siblings who share 50% of their DNA. But "semi-identical" twins are so rare that experts say they have only identified two cases so far. Formed by a single egg and two sperm, "semi-identical" twins share anywhere from 50% to 100% of their genomes.

316.

Almost half the world's seaborne trade passes through the Strait of Gibraltar, connecting the Mediterranean Sea to the Atlantic Ocean.

317.

Rayna Kasabova (1897-1969) was a Bulgarian Air Force nurse and the first woman in the world who participated in a military flight. At age of 15, during the First Balkan War in 1912, she joined the Bulgarian Air Force and flew above Edirne, Turkey, to throw out propaganda leaflets in Turkish.

318.

The oldest Roman lighthouse in use today is La Torre de Hercules located in Galicia, Spain. The structure was built in the 2nd century CE and renovated in 1791.

319.

Arthroscopic knee surgery is the number-one most common orthopaedic operation. More than two million are performed annually to clean ragged cartilage for people with arthritis and degenerative wear and tear in their knees, including torn meniscus. Yet sham surgery studies and other research have shown it offers no advantages for the vast majority of such patients. They would do just as well with physical therapy, weight loss, and exercise.

320.

In the movies of the "Mission Impossible" movies, each message auto destroys after five seconds.

321.

A dead humpback whale was found on the edge of the Amazon jungle in early 2019. Scientists are still unsure as to how exactly a whale ended up dead on the edge of the Amazon rainforest in Brazil, some 15 m (50 ft) from the ocean shore and close to the Amazon river mouth.

322.

In 1801, while making a star map, Italian priest and astronomer, Giuseppe Piazzi, accidentally discovered the first and largest asteroid, Ceres, orbiting between Mars and Jupiter.

323.

In 1714, Daniel Gabriel Fahrenheit, a German-born scientist who lived and worked primarily in the Netherlands, developed the first modern thermometer – the mercury thermometer, with more refined measurements than previous temperature gauges. Today, the Fahrenheit scale is used primarily in the United States and some Caribbean countries. The rest of the world uses the Celsius scale.

324.

There are only two double landlocked countries in the world. Liechtenstein is surrounded by two landlocked countries: Switzerland and Austria. Uzbekistan is surrounded by five, all of them ending with "stan": Afghanistan, Kazakhstan, Kyrgyzstan, Tajikistan, and Turkmenistan.

325.

San Marino has never won a medal at the Olympic Games.

326.

Australia has the largest claim of Antarctic territory: about 42% of Antarctica.

327.

The abbreviation ISBN you see on the back of every book means "International Standard Book Number".

328.

A *sphinx* is a mythical creature in Ancient Egypt and Greece with the head of a human and the body of a lion. In Greek tradition, the sphinx has the head of a human, the haunches of a lion, and sometimes the wings of a bird. Did you know that there is an entire family of sphinx moths that includes about 1,450 species?

329.

Freetown is the capital and largest city of
Sierra Leone. Libreville is the capital and largest city
of Gabon. Both African capitals have literally the same
name in English and French language, respectively.

330.

Nelson Bunker Hunt (1926-2014) was
an American oil company executive. He was a
billionaire whose fortune collapsed after he and his
brothers, William Herbert and Lamar Hunt,
tried to manipulate the world silver market. In the
1970s, Hunt and his brothers accumulated large
amounts of silver: 100 million troy ounces
(3,100,000 kg). That is why the price of silver rose
from $11 an ounce in September 1979 to $50 an
ounce in January 1980. Silver prices ultimately
collapsed to below $11 an ounce two months later.
The largest single-day drop in the price of silver
occurred on 27 March 1980, aka "Silver Thursday".
The Hunt brothers were charged with "manipulating
and attempting to manipulate the prices of silver
futures contracts and silver bullion during 1979 and
1980" by the United States Commodity Futures
Trading Commission, and in 1988,
they filed for bankruptcy.

331.

The Colosseum in Rome, Italy, is inhabited by hundreds of cats.

332.

Through the centuries, the Catholic Church in Rome has required that Catholics abstain from eating meat on Fridays during the year, as well as on Wednesdays and Fridays during Lent. In early 1966, Pope Paul VI urged that the practice of fasting and abstinence be adapted to local economic conditions. As a result, the vast majority of Catholics now eat meat on Friday.

333.

The highest and the lowest points in South America are both in Argentina.

334.

Asia was named after the Greek word "Asia" which was used to name the Persian Empire at the time.

335.

For Ancient Persians, telling the truth was very important and was part of their state religion, *Zoroastrianism*.

336.

On 20 July 1969, Neil Armstrong put his left foot on the Moon and created the first human footprint there.

337.

In the USA, only 1% of the top 1% believes coming from a rich family is essential to become rich.

338.

The mountainous city of Taif, near Mecca, is far cooler in the summer months than the official capital of Saudi Arabia, Riyadh. This is why Taif is the Saudi summer capital.

339.

The FBI built a secret mock town. *Hogan's Alley* is a tactical training facility of more than 40,000 m² (10 acres), operated by the Bureau's Training Academy, USA. It opened in 1987 and was designed to provide a realistic urban setting for training agents of the FBI, DEA, and other local and international law enforcement agencies. Hogan's Alley consists of a street with a bank, a post office, a hotel, a laundromat, a barbershop, a pool hall, homes, shops, and more, many of which are named after events in the FBI's past. The town is populated by actors who play parts appropriate to the training that is in progress; most play innocent bystanders, but some play terrorists, bank robbers, drug dealers, and other criminal roles. One of the buildings houses a classroom for training agents on-site, and another building houses a working FBI office used in some simulated scenarios.

340.

In 1995, during a football match in Zaragoza, Spain, between the local club and Chelsea (UK), bad blood was escalating between the two sets of supporters. It all changed when the local fans started chanting "Pisalo, pisalo!" This was interpreted as "Peace and love, peace and love!" by the Chelsea fans who, surprised, became peaceful and quiet. What was actually meant was "stamp on them!"

341.

Every year since 1932, the Netherlands has encouraged reading with *Boekenweek* (Book Week), a celebration of literature marked with literary festivals and book signings across the country. Traditionally, a well-known Dutch author writes a special novel, the "book week gift" or *Boekenweekgeschenk* – which is given out for free to people who buy books during the festivities or sign up to a library. Additionally, people get free rail travel across their country's entire network during the weekend if they show a book instead of a ticket.

342.

In the period 2008-2019, Aaron Ramsey was a football player for Arsenal, UK. He scored 40 goals for the team, and there was a rumour that each time he scores, a celebrity dies. Coincidence or not, 23 celebrities have died after a goal of his. The list includes Osama Bin Laden, Steve Jobs, Muammar Gaddafi, Whitney Houston, Paul Walker, Robin Williams, and David Bowie.

343.

The Philippines fly the national flag upside-down in time of war.

344.

Soviet cosmonaut, Sergei Krikalev, became known as
the last Soviet citizen because he was sent up to the
International Space Station from the USSR
in May 1991, only to return 310 days later,
in March 1992, to a different country, Russia.

345.

The *Lincoln Futura* is a concept car promoted by
Ford's Lincoln brand. First presented in 1955, the
Futura was later modified by George Barris into the
Batmobile, for the 1960s TV series Batman.

346.

The US fundamentalist Christian theme park *Ark Encounter* opened in 2016. It boasts a five-story-high replica of Noah's Ark. Ironically, in 2017, the replica was damaged by extensive rainfall, and the owners proceeded to sue the insurance company over rain damage.

347.

Cornelius "Commodore" Vanderbilt began his steamship and railroad empire (in New York, USA) in 1810 with $100 he borrowed from his mother. By the time he died in 1877, he was worth $100 million. Today (six generations later), the enterprises he founded are no longer in the family and the accumulated wealth is long gone.

348.

The last duel with swords in France took place in 1967 between French politicians, Gaston Defferre and René Ribière. While the Vietnam War was raging, rock and roll was taking over the world, and men were exploring space, those two Frenchmen decided to settle their differences with a good old-fashioned duel.

349.

Unlike Japanese or Chinese alphabets, which have thousands of characters and each can have 10, 15 or more strokes, the most complex Korean character has only five strokes.

350.

Finnish Jews fought in the Finnish Army during WW2. Finland was an ally of Nazi Germany.

351.

In 2019, a 3-foot-tall silver bunny set an art world record. Rabbit, by the controversial artist Jeff Koons, was sold for more than $91 million at Christie's Auction House – the highest ever amount for a work by a living artist sold at an auction.

352.

From the year 2700 onwards, the celebration of Easter for the Eastern Orthodox Church and the Catholic Church will never coincide again. The last time Easter celebrations will coincide is estimated to be in 2698.

353.

The *Ivy League* is a US collegiate athletic conference comprising sports teams from eight private universities in the North-eastern United States: Brown University, Columbia University, Cornell University, Dartmouth College, Harvard University, the University of Pennsylvania, Princeton University, and Yale University. It is not widely known, however, that from the 1940s through to the 1970s, all incoming freshmen (including US Presidents, Donald Trump and George W. Bush) were photographed nude, ostensibly as a part of a study on body types and social hierarchy. What remained of the images were destroyed between 1995 and 2001.

354.

In June 2019, a flight from Manchester, UK, was delayed by almost eight hours after a passenger mistakenly opened an emergency exit instead of the toilet door, thus deploying the evacuation slide.

355.

Twins are twice as likely to be left-handed as the rest of the population.

356.

It takes more time to pronounce the abbreviation WWW than it takes to say "World Wide Web".

357.

In 2009, villagers in Ukraine's district of Chernovitska noticed various spots miraculously appearing on the walls of a local pub. News spread and numerous worshipers from Ukraine and neighbouring Romania and Moldova came in pilgrimage to what they perceived to be "self-made icons" of the Holy Mother and Jesus. Many brought flowers and lit candles, and others kissed the walls. However, chemical analysis proved that the origin of these "drawings" was much more trivial – local drunks had repeatedly urinated on the walls, thus bleaching the paint in random shapes.

358.

During the plague in the 14th century (aka
the Black Death), economic inequality in Europe was
at an all-time low.

359.

William Hedgecock Webster is the only person so far
who has served as Director of the Federal Bureau of
Investigation (FBI), and then as Director of Central
Intelligence (CIA) of the USA.

360.

The Kingdom of Sikkim was founded in the
17th century. Ruled by a Buddhist priest-king, known
as the *Chogyal*, it had the highest per capita income
and literacy rate among all Himalayan states. In 1975,
the Indian military deposed the monarchy and Sikkim
became the 22nd state of India.

361.

Andorra declared war on Germany in WWI in 1914
but never sent any troops into the conflict. As Andorra
did not fight in WWI, they were not even invited to
sign the Treaty of Versailles, and until 1957, Andorra
was technically at war with Austria and Germany!

362.

The *Sismo Detector* is a smartphone app which effectively alerts Peruvians that a potentially dangerous earthquake may occur.

363.

In 2011, the tiny Indian Ocean island of Mayotte became France's 101st department with the ability to send MPs to the French Parliament. However, Mayotte was forced to repudiate Islamic law in favour of the French rule of law which outlaws, for example, parallel sharia courts, polygamy, forced marriages, and gives rights to women to testify in court.

364.

Nobuo Fujita was an officer of the Imperial Japanese Navy who flew a floatplane from a submarine aircraft carrier during World War II. He remains the only pilot in history to have bombed (in 1942) the contiguous USA during wartime.

365.

Major-General Chaim Herzog served as the sixth President of Israel in the period 1983-1993. Worldwide, he is so far the only head of a military intelligence service to have become a head of state.

366.

The "Truck Driver Face" is the result of sun damage after years behind the wheel driving a truck. The damage is typically limited to the left side of the face since the position of the driver's side window leaves this side more exposed to the sun's harsh rays.

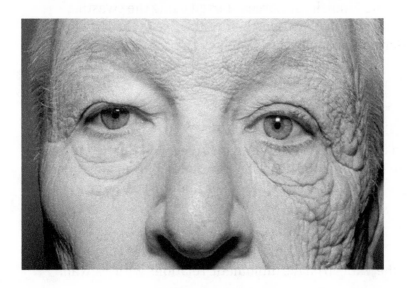

367.

In 2017, scientists discovered an underwater "city" off the east coast of Australia, built entirely by octopuses. The molluscs were observed to flirt, mate, and fight over the best homes.

368.

As of early 2018, China's CCTV surveillance network comprises about 200 million surveillance cameras and counting.

369.

The Finnish Air Forces started using the swastika symbol in 1918, well before the rise of the Nazi in Germany. However, Finland was forced to drop it after World War II's end, as it closely resembled the Nazi symbol.

370.

In 2016, Burma sentenced a 30-year-old Dutch tourist to three months in prison for unplugging an amplifier broadcasting a late-night Buddhist sermon.

371.

As of 2019, only seventeen countries (plus the Vatican) have diplomatic relations with Taiwan.

372.

Sirimavo Bandaranaike became Prime Minister of Ceylon (nowadays known as Sri Lanka) in 1960. She was the first female head of government in the modern world.

373.

Europe-wide, the oldest city is Plovdiv, Bulgaria, settled around 6000 BCE.

374.

On 27 June 1969, Honduras and El Salvador played a 1970 FIFA World Cup qualifier football game. The same day, El Salvador dissolved all diplomatic ties with Honduras, and within two weeks started the so-called *Football War* (or the *100 Hours War*).

375.

Bananas are slightly radioactive.

376.

Most cruise ships have a designated morgue in case a passenger passes away during a sailing.

377.

Salar de Uyuni is the world's largest salt flat, at 10,582 sq. km (4,086 sq mi). It is located in southwest Bolivia at an elevation of 3,656 meters (11,995 ft) above sea level.

378.
The *Tenere Tree* was a solitary acacia that was once considered the most isolated tree on Earth, the only one for over 400 kilometres (250 mi). It was knocked down in 1973 by a drunk truck driver.

CHAPTER III

Disturbing facts about our world

1.

Support for an increase in the minimum salary is naturally the highest among minimum salary workers. However, it is the lowest among those who just get a bit more than the minimum salary.

2.

In 2012, Latvia became the last country of the European Union to abolish capital punishment in wartime. Europe-wide (as of early 2018), only Belarus foresees the death penalty for peacetime crimes, while the death penalty for wartime crimes exists in Belarus and Kazakhstan.

3.

In 2018, a 1-year-old boy who was separated from his family was forced to appear in front of an immigration judge in Arizona, USA. The judge asked the child whether he understood the proceedings. Eventually, the child was granted a voluntary departure order so that he could be reunited with his family in Honduras.

4.

Until 2011, many chickens in the USA were fed arsenic.

5.

The Polish resistance fighter, Witold Pilecki, fought in the Polish-Soviet War of 1919-1921, against the Nazi invasion in 1939, volunteered to enter as a spy into the concentration camp Auschwitz in 1940, and took part in the Warsaw Uprising in 1944. He survived all that only to be killed by the Communist regime in 1947.

6.

Although Japan has been a signatory to the United Nations International Convention on the Elimination of All Forms of Racial Discrimination since 1995, it – like the United States – does not criminalise
hate speech.

7.

In the United States of America, over 60 percent of firearm deaths are suicides.
Suicides kill more people than all forms of violence, including homicide, terrorism, armed conflict and executions, combined.

8.

In early 2018, Jack Robison, a judge in Texas, USA, interrupted the jury saying that God told him the defendant was not guilty. The jury nevertheless returned a "guilty" verdict.

9.

In 2010, the most massive microfinance crisis worldwide erupted in the Indian state of Andhra Pradesh. The crisis caused a wave of hundreds of suicides.

10.

Some tattoo inks are produced with animal products, such as bone char, glycerine from animal fat, gelatin from hooves, or shellac from beetles.

11.

The youngest Vietnam War US Marine, Dan Bullock, was 14 years old when he enlisted. He was killed in action at the age of 15.

12.

The Rosenbergs are so far the only US citizens executed in peacetime for treason. Julius and Ethel Rosenberg were sentenced to death in the early 1950s for passing atomic secrets to the Soviets.

13.

The notorious Nazi, Joseph Goebbels, spoke quite eloquently against disabled people. However, he had a deformed right leg and due to his deformity, was rejected for military service in World War I.

14.

Alva Campbell (1948-2018) was a death row inmate from Ohio, USA. During his execution in 2017, the executioners were unable to find a suitable vein to insert the needle for the lethal injection. His execution was rescheduled for 2019, but he died of natural causes before that.

15.

The German town of Mödlareuth is still divided some thirty years after the Berlin Wall fell. It still has two mayors, two telephone areas and postcodes, two vehicle registration codes, belongs simultaneously to two different municipalities, and its residents vote in two different states (Bavaria and Thuringia).

16.

The leading causes of death in the world's twenty richest countries are as follows: heart disease, stroke, lung cancer, suicide, Alzheimer's, and cirrhosis.

17.

Grigory Kulik was the only Soviet Marshal to be executed after World War II during Stalin's post-war purges. Considered by many historians a weak military commander, Kulik was opposed to the use of tanks, minefields, submachine guns, and the emblematic *Katyusha* rocket artillery system.

18.

According to a study from 2017, 90% of French women have been harassed sexually while using public transport.

19.

10,000 soldiers were killed on the very last day of World War I.

20.

You can marry a dead person in France. You only need to prove that the deceased had serious intentions to marry you.

21.

Crucifixion is one of the official methods of execution in Sudan, Iran, United Arab Emirates,
and Saudi Arabia.

22.

Since 2007, over a dozen severed feet still inside their shoes have washed up on the beaches of the Pacific coast of Canada. Their origin remains a mystery.

23.

The Frenchman Tarrare (1772-1798) had truly unusual eating habits. Always hungry, he would swallow corks, stones, live animals, and a whole basketful of apples. He worked as a street performer, eating in public live cats, snakes, lizards, and puppies, and swallowed eels whole without chewing.

24.

McDonald's' employee health page *McResource Line*, which is now shut down, once warned against eating McDonald's burgers and fries. The same website advised employees to apply for food stamps, pawn their belongings, and find second jobs if their salary was not enough.

25.

In ancient China and Japan, "laughing" was used as a method for torture by making a goat lick the captive's legs. Abusive tickling is capable of provoking extreme physiological reactions in the victim, such as vomiting, incontinence (losing control of bladder), and loss of consciousness due to an inability to breathe.

26.

The quest for extreme selfies killed 259 people between 2011 and 2017, a 2018 US National Library of Medicine study has revealed.

27.

Since early 2019, Saudi women have been notified via SMS when their husbands decide to divorce. The measure is expected to end what are known as *secret divorces* – cases where men end a marriage without telling their wives.

28.

Mao Zedong, the first communist leader of China, tried to improve China's agriculture in the 1950s by encouraging people to kill sparrows but ended up starving tens of millions to death. The elimination of sparrows from the food chain led to increased insect populations, which ate even more human food, and contributed to the *Great Chinese Famine*.

29.

The interior of the Pinkas Synagogue in Prague, Czech
Republic, is painted with the names of all Jewish
Czechs killed during World War II. It is thought to be
the longest gravestone inscription containing
77,297 names.

30.

In four countries worldwide, women cannot register a
business. In eighteen countries, a husband can stop
his wife from working.

31.

Derek Kieper from Nebraska, USA, was so passionate about the idea that seatbelt laws violated his liberties, he wrote an opinion column about it in 2004. A few months later, he died in a car accident. Two of his friends in the car survived.

They were wearing seatbelts.

32.

In Victorian England, rich people organised "Egyptian-themed" parties that involved the unwrapping of a real mummified corpse. They called these events *mummy unwrapping parties* or *unrollings.*

33.

A train with 5,000 tons of human faeces was abandoned in the US town of Parrish, Alabama. The human waste was sitting in more than 200 rail cars for two months before it was eventually disposed of in April 2018.

34.

The majority of the states in the USA require would-be government contractors to sign an oath, promising they will not boycott Israel.

35.

The *No Fly List* is a list created and maintained by the United States federal government's Terrorist Screening Center of people who are prohibited from boarding commercial aircraft for travel within, into, or out of the United States. It is presently listing well above one million names and creates many false positive alerts. Sometimes, it affects toddlers sharing the same name as a suspected terrorist or even politicians or Armed Forces personnel.

36.

Jerome Irving Rodale earned a fortune as the publisher of numerous health-food books and "Prevention" magazine. During a taping of *The Dick Cavett Show* that never aired, the 72-year-old Rodale allegedly told the host that "I never felt better in my life" and that he intended to live to 100. He died of a heart attack during the show.

37.

Two US nuns stole 500,000 US dollars from St Joseph's Catholic School in Redondo Beach, California, over several years until 2018. They used some of the money to go gambling in Las Vegas. Yet, the Archdiocese of Los Angeles would not press criminal charges.

38.

During the civil war of 68-69 CE in Ancient Rome, the troops of Emperor Vespasian captured and sacked the city of Cremona for four full days, killing and raping literally everyone inside the city walls.

39.

The *Nanking Massacre* or the *Rape of Nanking* was an episode of mass murder and mass rape committed by Imperial Japanese troops against the residents of the then capital of the Republic of China, during the Second Sino-Japanese War. During the period of six weeks starting on 13 December 1937, Japanese soldiers killed Chinese civilians and disarmed combatants, who numbered an estimated 40,000 to over 300,000, and perpetrated widespread rape and looting.

40.

Seven out of the ten bloodiest wars were fought in China.

41.

In 2013, a Russian artist named Pyotr Pavlensky nailed his genitals to the pavement in Red Square in Moscow as an act of protest aimed at "the police state".

42.

The famous South Korean film director, Shin Sang-ok, and his wife, the actress Choi Eun-hee, were abducted in North Korea between in 1978. After three years in prison, Shin was united with Choi, and the two were instructed by the leader of North Korea, Kim Jong-Il, to make films for him and boost the local film industry. After making many films for North Korea, in 1986, Choi and Shin managed to escape to a US embassy while in Vienna, Austria.

43.

For humankind, the three deadliest animals are mosquito, human, and snake. In this order.

44.

In the USA, nine billion chickens are raised and killed for food each year. This makes about one million every hour.

45.

On 13 May 1945, a German deserter execution occurred five days after the capitulation of Nazi Germany in World War II, when an illegal court-martial, composed of the captured and disarmed German officers kept under Allied guard in Amsterdam, Netherlands, imposed a death sentence upon two German deserters: Bruno Dorfer and Rainer Beck. The mock trial occurred in a prisoner-of-war camp run by the Canadian Army. The Nazi German prisoners of war formed a firing squad, which carried out the sentence, supplied with rifles by the Canadians.

46.

The leading cause of death of people in the Ancient Roman arenas was "mauling by wild beasts".

47.

Several 2018 studies showed that a US white man with a criminal record has a slightly better chance to be hired than a black one without.

48.

In 1992, a US father injected his baby boy with a HIV-infected syringe to avoid paying alimony. The child, named Bryan Jackson, survived so far against all odds, while the father is in prison for life.

49.

On 2 October 2018, the Saudi journalist, Jamal Khashoggi, entered the Saudi consulate in Istanbul, Turkey. Saudi agents killed him inside the consulate, and his dismembered body was taken out of the building disguised as diplomatic mail.

50.

In the 18th century England, people could enter London Zoo without having to pay the entrance fee – all they had to do was to bring some cats or dogs to feed the always hungry lions.

51.

In 2014, three teen burglars snorted a grandpa's ashes instead of cocaine in St. Peters, Missouri, USA. They broke into a house and stole cash and various items, including a box with ashes, which the thieves mistook for cocaine.

52.

Emmett Louis Till (1941-1955) was an African-American who was lynched in Mississippi, USA, at the age of 14, after being accused of flirting with a white woman (Carolyn Bryant). Her husband, Roy Bryant, with the help of J.W. Milam abducted, tortured, and killed Emmett. In September 1955, they were acquitted by an all-white jury of Emmett's kidnapping and murder. Protected against double jeopardy, the two men publicly admitted in a 1956 interview with Look magazine that they had indeed murdered the boy. The brutality of the crime and the fact that the killers remained unpunished made Emmett Till posthumously an icon of the Civil Rights Movement.

53.

In 2015, a car hit a 6-year-old child in Pernik, Bulgaria. In 2018, the court decided that a running child could bump into the side of a moving car, and acquitted the driver of the SUV.

54.

Poor US kids who have above-average academic results are less likely to graduate from college than richer kids who have worse-than-average marks.

55.

In 17th-century London, UK, tourists paid for guided tours of Bedlam Mental Hospital, enjoying the spectacle of the inmates, some in the last days of their dementia.

56.

In 2017, a Malaysian spiritual magician died while performing a ritual that was supposed to "cleanse body and soul". This happened after he accidentally steamed himself to death in a stainless steel wok where he habitually sat surrounded by rice, sweet corn, and vegetarian buns. The 68-year-old guru, Lim Ba, had been performing human steaming for more than a decade despite family objections.

57.

The British King William the Conqueror died in 1087.
He was a big man and by the time his funeral was
organised, his body was bloated with gas.
The sarcophagus was too short, so they tried to
squeeze the corpse into it, but
the dead monarch exploded.

58.

Since early 2019, Saudi men can use a government-run app to get texts telling them about the movements of their wives and daughters. The app also allows men to cancel travel and restrict women from flying out of certain airports.

59.

A number of Belgians who collaborated with
the Nazi regime were promised a pension for
their "fidelity, loyalty, and obedience".
A staggering 38,000 Belgians have received the
pension from the German state since the end of WWII.
As of 2019, twenty-seven Belgians continue to receive
between €425 and €1,275 ($500 to $1,500)
per month from the German state.

60.

In 1949, the Fernald State School, originally called *The Massachusetts School for the Feeble-Minded*, organised a "Science Club" and many boy students wanted to become members. It turned out that scientists from Harvard University and the Massachusetts Institute of Technology fed radioactive milk to a group of boys who had been led to believe that they were joining a "science club". The Fernald students' experiment was just one among dozens of radiation experiments approved by the Atomic Energy Commission. Between 1945 and 1962, more than 210,000 civilians and soldiers were exposed to radiation, often without knowing it. What seems unthinkable in today's era of ethics review boards and informed consent was standard procedure at the dawn of the Atomic Age.

61.

Emile Alphonse Griffith (1938-2013) was a professional boxer from the US Virgin Islands who became a World Champion. His best-known contest was a 1962 title match with the Cuban Benny Paret. At the weigh-in, Paret infuriated Griffith, a bisexual man, by touching his buttocks and making homosexual slurs. Griffith won the fight by knockout, eventually killing Paret.

62.

In a despicable yet weird homophobic incident from early 2019, a shorthaired Bulgarian woman was attacked by a guy for "looking like a gay man".

63.

In early 2019, Russia's Justice Ministry proposed exempting officials in "exceptional circumstances" from anti-corruption regulations in the new draft legislation, following a plan set by Russian President, Vladimir Putin. The amendments seek to exempt officials from legal accountability when violating anti-corruption rules is "unavoidable".

64.

In the early 1980s, some 20,000 people from central Spain were reported ill from *Toxic Oil Syndrome*. By the end of 1997, the death toll reached 1,800 cases. The officially held theory was that adulterated industrial oil was imported illegally from France in 1981, re-refined, and subsequently sold for human consumption in Spain. However, other studies pointed to the use of a pesticide containing organophosphates on the tomatoes grown in the region of Almeria in southern Spain.

65.

In 1959, John Howard Griffin did a crazy experiment: to comprehend the lives of black people in the southern US states, he darkened his skin to become black. As the civil rights movement tested various forms of civil disobedience, Griffin travelled from New Orleans to Atlanta. His book, "Black Like Me", sold more than 10 million copies and led to a successful lecture circuit across the country. It also led to Griffin being hanged in effigy in his hometown, his parents receiving death threats, his wife and children fleeing to Mexico, and Griffin himself being beaten severely by the Ku Klux Klan.

66.

Players in escape room games are locked inside a room or building and must solve puzzles and find clues that lead them to the key to get out of the escape room. Regarded as an intellectual challenge, the games are highly popular among teenagers in many countries. In early 2019, Polish officials shut down many escape room entertainment venues for safety flaws, following a fire in one establishment that killed five teenage girls.

67.

Bloody Sunday was a sequence of events that took place in Bydgoszcz, a Polish city with a sizable German minority, between 3 and 4 September 1939, during the German invasion of Poland. German *Selbstschutz* (German for "self-protection") snipers fired on retreating Polish troops; the Polish reacted by executing ethnic Germans and, after the fall of the city, approximately 600-800 Polish hostages were shot in a mass execution as "revenge" by the German Army and militia. The term "Bloody Sunday" was created and supported by Nazi propaganda officials.

68.

Obesity kills three times as many people as malnutrition.

69.

In 1962, two American scientists, David Bernays and Charles Sawyer, tried to warn the residents of Yungay, Peru, of a possible massive avalanche. The government ordered them to retract their report or face prison, and they fled the country. In 1970, an avalanche completely destroyed the town.

70.

In 2010, Slovak security services at the Poprad-Tatry Airport planted plastic explosives in a passenger's baggage for dog training purposes and then forgot to remove them. The passenger landed safely at Dublin Airport, Ireland, and due to miscommunication, it was only three days later when the Irish police tracked him down and recovered the explosives.

71.

In 2019, an Indian voter chopped off his index finger after realising he had voted for the "wrong" political party. Pawan Kumar accidentally voted for another party, confused by the many symbols
on the voting machine.

72.

People with mental handicaps in the USA are currently estimated to number over eight million.

73.

In 2008, the store chain Lidl in the Czech Republic became notorious for an internal document in one store, according to which the employed women were supposed to wear visible headbands at the time of menstruation. This would allow them to go to the bathroom more often.

74.

Ethiopia's re-education camps re-opened in late 2018. The pattern of mass arrests followed by "re-education" has a long history in the country. Thousands were sent to camps after demonstrations against disputed election results in 2005. Tens of thousands were detained during a state of emergency imposed in 2016 to curtail protests against the ruling party. Military officers lectured them on subjects, including the "Ethiopian Renaissance", the perils of neoliberalism, and the supposed threat of Western-sponsored "colour revolutions".

75.

In May 2019, a "traffic jam" of some 320 alpinists trying to climb Everest created significant delays for those going up and down. As a result, three climbers died.

CHAPTER IV

Facts about human and animal sexuality

1.

NASA confirmed that in space, the sexual positions "reverse cowgirl" and "doggy style" are the same thing.

2.

Bonobos do not form permanent monogamous sexual relationships with individual partners. They also do not seem to discriminate in their sexual behaviour by sex or age. When bonobos come upon a new food source, the increased excitement will usually lead to communal sexual activity, presumably decreasing tension and encouraging peaceful feeding.

3.

In 2019, Taiwan became the first Asian country to legalise same-sex marriage. At the same time, the tiny sultanate of Brunei introduced a new, stricter Islamic law, making anal sex and adultery offences punishable by death by stoning (*lapidation*).

4.

A UK transgender person was jailed in a women's prison in 2018. Karen White, born Stephen Terence Wood, admitted sexually assaulting women in prison and raping another two women outside jail. Eventually, Karen/Stephen was sentenced to life in (this time male) prison.

5.

In 2019, a Kuwaiti therapist and academic, Dr Mariam Al-Sohel, announced she could cure homosexuality with an anal suppository.
The medication is supposed to
"kill the parasitic anal worm feeding on semen".

6.

Cameroon holds the sad record of the highest percentage of both men and women who report having been victims of forced sex as children.

7.

In 2018, Angela Ponce participated in the
67th Miss Universe pageant. While she did not win,
the 27-year-old Spanish beauty became
the first transgender woman to ever participate
in the international competition.

8.

Sea slugs are not the only animals who abandon their penis. However, the *Chromodoris reticulata* is the first creature known that can re-grow its appendage – and its disposable penis gives it a sexual advantage.

9.

An IKEA discount code was revealed when peed on by pregnant women. An ad from 2018 featured a popular item – a crib – and the message "Peeing on this ad may change your life". The ad doubled as a pregnancy test. And if the ad determined the adventurous reader was pregnant, then the positive pregnancy test/ad would reveal a discount coupon.

10.

The word "vanilla" is derived from the Latin word "vagina", meaning "sheath, scabbard".

11.

The *Four Corners Monument* is a point in the USA where Utah, Colorado, Arizona, and New Mexico all meet. It is the only place in the US where you can be in four states at the same time. It is also the only place that you can have sex in four different states at one time, and many people get arrested every year trying.

12.

Jamie Shupe became the first legally non-binary gender person in the USA in 2016.

13.

Diego the tortoise, aged 100, has fathered around 800 offspring on his native Galapagos Archipelago, helping to save his species from extinction in the process.

14.

The *gay panic defence* is a legal defence usually attempted against charges of assault or murder. A defendant claims they acted in a state of violent temporary insanity because of unwanted same-sex sexual advances. In 2008, Joseph Biedermann stabbed Terrance Hauser to death in Hoffman Estates, Illinois, USA and was later on acquitted using such defence.

15.

According to a 2016 study, a woman with very high intelligence will be less appealing to men than an equally attractive woman, but only slightly above average intelligent. Men are less attracted to intelligent women because the comparison with their own intelligence damages men's egos.

16.
A Bosnian couple decided to divorce in 2007 when they found out that both of them had been having an online affair. The ironic part was that the couple were actually having an affair with each other.

17.
Long penises help hermit crabs avoid being robbed during sex, as it allows the male crab to procreate without leaving his shell – reducing the risk of it being stolen while he is busy.

18.
Following repeated thefts, Washington State, USA, changed "Mile 420" and "Mile 69" signs with "Mile 68.9" and Mile "419.9" respectively. The number "69" alludes to a sexual act, and "420" serves as popular shorthand for smoking marijuana.

19.
Since 2018, one of the leading porn websites, *Pornhub*, has been releasing videos with closed captioning in an attempt to help its deaf and hard-of-hearing viewers and make its site more "inclusive".

20.

On dating sites, men care mostly about women's weight, and women care mostly about men's height and income.

21.

On the walls of Cologne City Hall, Germany, hidden under a larger statue of Archbishop Konrad von Hochstaden, there is a carving showing a man giving oral sex to himself. It dates around 1410, and no one knows why it is there.

22.

Lactose-intolerant people, listen up: quite often, natural latex condoms contain dairy products such as *casein*.

23.

Up to now, the Peruvian Lina Marcela Medina de Jurado (born in 1933) is the youngest confirmed mother in medical history. She gave birth at the age of 5 years, 7 months, and 21 days.

24.

In 2006, three US men tried to dig up a young woman's dead body to have sex with it. Their charges of attempted sexual assault were dismissed because, at the time, there was no law against necrophilia in Wisconsin, USA.

25.

Moon cup (aka menstrual cup) is a feminine hygiene product that is inserted into the vagina during menstruation. Its purpose is to prevent the menstrual fluid (blood from uterine lining) from leaking onto clothes. Menstrual cups are usually made of flexible medical grade silicone and shaped like a bell with a stem.

26.

In January 2019, the German city of Hanover re-formulated all administrative texts to become gender-neutral. The city claimed to be taking into account the "multiplicity of sexual identities".

27.

In 2016, South African Health Minister, Aaron Motsoaledi, banned "doggy style" sex as it supposedly caused cancer and stroke.

28.

Polish scientists created an exciting tool to help with male infertility. Announced in January 2019, it is called CoolMen and is essentially a testicle cooler.

29.

In early 2019, the prominent US "gay conversion therapist", David Matheson, divorced his wife and came out as gay. He was a leading member of an "ex-gay movement" that has been widely discredited by medical professionals.

30.

Brothels in Switzerland have recently started training employees to use defibrillators after a series of fatal incidents.

31.

Huichol Indians are descendants of the Aztecs and live in the mountains of north-central Mexico. During traditional childbirth, the father sits above his labouring wife on the roof of their hut. Ropes are tied around his testicles, and his wife holds onto the other ends. Each time she feels a painful contraction, she tugs on the ropes so that her husband will share some of the pain of their child's entrance into the world.

32.

There have been cases of men getting their penis stuck in various weird places. The crazy locations include bottles, pipes, benches, vacuum cleaners, subway gates, dumbbells, etc.

33.

Shi Pei Pu (1938-2009) was a Chinese opera singer from Beijing, China. He became a spy who obtained secrets from Bernard Boursicot, an employee at the French Embassy, during a 20-year-long sexual affair in which the performer convinced the Frenchman that he was a woman.

34.

There have been several reported cases where a woman had sex with identical twins and got pregnant. The result is that no DNA test can prove who the father is.

35.

In 2015, a US swingers' club was about to open in Nashville, Tennessee. Local lawmakers amended the zoning for the area, in effect, blocking the club from opening. The owner successfully dodged it by declaring the club a church.

36.

Up until 1973, homosexuality was considered a
mental illness in the United States.

37.

Female ferrets need to have sex at least once a year,
otherwise die of estrogen poisoning.

38.

In early 2019, Danish politician, Joachim B. Olsen, put
an ad on the popular porn-streaming website
Pornhub ahead of the country's upcoming general
elections. It roughly reads: "When you are done
masturbating, vote for Joachim".

39.

Transgender athletes may only compete in the Olympic Games if they have undergone sex reassignment surgery before puberty.

40.

In medieval France, if a wife filed for divorce, claiming that her husband was impotent, the husband had to undergo some humiliating tests. He had to, for instance, have an erection and ejaculate in front of the jury.

41.

A French company was found liable for the death of an employee who had a cardiac arrest while having sex with a stranger on a business trip. The man, named as Xavier X, was working as an engineer for TSO, a railway services company based near Paris. He died at a hotel during a trip to central France in 2013, as a result of what the employer called "an extramarital relationship with a perfect stranger". In 2019, a Paris court ruled that his death was an industrial accident and that the family was entitled to compensation.

42.

In many mammal species, the female does not have to consent for sex to happen. Due to anatomical peculiarities, however, the female elephants and hyenas cannot be raped.

###

VERIFICATION PROCESS

To start with, however a great read Wikipedia is, I have never used it to confirm facts; I instead checked the sources listed there and evaluated them.

Anything science-related like "Redheads can produce their supply of Vitamin D" would need to be confirmed by at least two (preferably three) separate scientific publications, be it on paper or online of the sort of https://www.genome.gov/education/, http://www.science.gov/, http://www.nasa.gov/, http://www.britannica.com/, http://nautil.us/, http://www.sciencemag.org/, https://www.nationalgeographic.com/, https://www.statnews.com/, https://www.wired.com/, https://undark.org/, https://www.newscientist.com/, http://www.howstuffworks.com/. The scientific publications and websites of the best universities worldwide are also consistently checked (excerpt from the list): University of Cambridge, Stanford University, University of Oxford, California Institute of Technology, Massachusetts Institute of Technology, Harvard University, Princeton University, Imperial College London, ETH Zurich – Swiss Federal Institute of Technology, Yale University, Columbia University, University of Toronto, Humboldt University of Berlin, University of Tokyo, Heidelberg University, University of Melbourne, Peking University etc.

For events or facts of the type "The French Fencing Federation recognised lightsabre duelling as a sport in early 2019", I checked at least three reputable newspaper articles and confirmed television reports. Example for newspapers/TV channels used to verify events: The New York Times, Washington Post, Wall Street Journal, The Guardian, The Economist, Financial Times, Times of India, Le Monde, The Sydney Morning Herald, Frankfurter Allgemeine Zeitung, Bloomberg, Al Jazeera, Reuters, Associated Press, BBC, TV5 MONDE, CNN, etc.

ACKNOWLEDGEMENTS

This book is dedicated to my family: my loving wife, Anna, my curious and restless sons, Pavel and Nikolay, and my mother, Maria, who sparked my interest in reading. Thank you for being so patient with me during the lengthy process of writing. You are my inspiration!

Many thanks to my editor, Andrea Leitenberger, to all test readers, friends, and colleagues who provided vital feedback and constructive criticism.

ZEALOUS TEST READERS:

Alexandra Oliveira-Jones
Brian Power
Eva Goulas
Heather Wilkinson
Istvan Kovacs
Jan Van Hecke
Kathy Tanghe
Linda Van Ras
Marina Heda
Robert Pernetta

ABOUT THE AUTHOR

Born in Bulgaria, I have lived in places like Germany, Belgium, and Iraq, before settling down with my family in Luxembourg. With varied interests, I have always suffered from an insatiable appetite for facts stemming from an unrestrainable intellectual curiosity. It has undoubtedly influenced my academic background and career: after acquiring Master degrees in Greek Philology, German and English Translation, I graduated in Crisis Management and Diplomacy, and most recently undertook an MBA. Member of MENSA.

My career has been equally broad and diverse, swinging from that of an army paratrooper and a military intelligence analyst; through to that of a civil servant with the European Commission, and presently, that of a clerk, performing purely financial tasks in a major bank.

My hobbies include scuba diving, travelling, and learning foreign languages.

CONNECT WITH THE AUTHOR

Email: **n.kostov@raiseyourbrain.com**

Facebook: **www.facebook.com/raiseyourbrain/**

Twitter: **@RaiseYourBrain**

Blog: **www.RaiseYourBrain.com**

FOLLOW ME ON GOODREADS:

goodreads   Home   My Books   Browse ▾

#1 most followed
#45 best reviewers
#2 top librarians
#64 top reviewers

OTHER BOOKS AVAILABLE ON AMAZON:

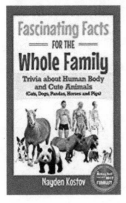

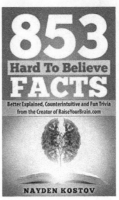

I hope you have enjoyed this book. I would greatly appreciate it if you write your honest **review** on Amazon and/or on GoodReads.com

***